Presented To:

Sandra Ranschaut
562-653-7023

From:

Barbara Fitzpatrick

Date:

12-30-12

VISIONS
of
HEAVEN

DESTINY IMAGE BOOKS BY ROBERTS LIARDON

The Azusa Street Revival

Frank Bartleman's Azusa Street

Smith Wigglesworth on Prayer, Power and Miracles

VISIONS
of
HEAVEN

4 Stories of People Who Have Seen the
After-Life

Roberts Liardon

DESTINY IMAGE® PUBLISHERS, INC.
P.O. Box 310, Shippensburg, PA 17257-0310
"Promoting Inspired Lives."

Previously published as *We Saw Heaven* by Destiny Image
Previous ISBN: 978-0-7684-2381-5

This book and all other Destiny Image, Revival Press, MercyPlace, Fresh Bread, Destiny Image Fiction, and Treasure House books are available at Christian bookstores and distributors worldwide.

For a U.S. bookstore nearest you, call 1-800-722-6774.
For more information on foreign distributors, call 717-532-3040.
Reach us on the Internet: www.destinyimage.com.

ISBN 13 TP: 978-0-7684-0297-1
ISBN 13 Ebook: 978-0-7684-8792-3

For Worldwide Distribution, Printed in the U.S.A.
1 2 3 4 5 6 7 8 / 16 15 14 13 12

CONTENTS

PART III *REBECCA SPRINGER*

PART IV *H.A. BAKER*

FOREWORD

ROBERTS LIARDON'S LIFE AND MINISTRY are having a powerful impact on the Body of Christ and appear to be poised to reach a new level in their influence for the Lord's last-day ministry.

As I've preached for his growing church, with the students of his Bible school attending, I sense something special is moving upon them. It could partially be from the influence of the dreams that he describes in this book, virtually enmeshing his life from a child. He is a strong Bible preacher and teacher, also a gatherer of materials of noted men and women of God of the past 100 years in an effort to reveal how God does His mighty deeds.

It is my feeling as Roberts continues to obey God, grow in the Word, build his strong teaching, and persevere, totally committed to the Lord Jesus, his impact will be immeasurable on thousands worldwide.

Sincerely,
Oral Roberts
(Written in 2000)

Part I

ROBERTS LIARDON

Chapter One

VISIONS ARE FOR TODAY!

WHEN I WAS EIGHT YEARS old, my life was, I think, fairly ordinary in most respects. Eight-year-old boys are not consumed with jobs or making a car payment or planning their retirement fund. Instead, their days revolve around school, their friends and pets, their favorite sports, and their families.

My own life was much the same, living in American's "heartland." I enjoyed meeting up with my friends to play sports. The summer I was eight, I remember rushing indoors from a baseball game and hurrying through my chores so that I could get back outside to more baseball! And yet, there are some aspects of my existence that were definitely far from average and certainly out of the ordinary.

When I was eight years old, I visited Heaven.

"Train Up a Child"

I was born February 14, 1966, in Tulsa, Oklahoma. My parents had moved there so that my mother could attend the charter class of 1965 at Oral Roberts University (ORU). I was born while she was attending ORU, and because I was the first baby boy born to a student, I was named Kenneth Roberts Liardon.

ORU Founder and then-President Oral Roberts and his wife, Evelyn, wanted the privilege of helping name the first boy and the first girl who were born to students of what was at that time a new university. I have always been proud of my name because of its origin.

When I was between five and six years old, my father left us and divorced my mother, and I did not see him again for many years. My grandmother, an Assembly of God pastor, then came to live with us. She had pastored for many years alongside my grandfather. Together, they had started more than 20 churches, mainly country Pentecostal congregations, during their ministry together.

My grandfather had died when I was about one year old. After that, Grandmother came to Tulsa to help raise my sister, Priscilla, and me in order that my mother could finish school and still work to support us.

What I remember most about those childhood years was all the prayer and study of the Bible that occurred in our home. These things were a central part of our lives. We had more prayer at home than we did at church! I have often said that there was more spiritual activity—more healings, and more power and evidence of God—in our front room than at some churches.

I don't say these things to be critical or derogatory. These are simply the facts. I believe we saw healings and answers to prayer because there was so much awareness of God in our home.

Both my mother and my grandmother spent time with my sister and me, training us in the "way we should go" (see Prov. 22:6). Grandmother, however, was able to spend more time with

Priscilla and me than our mother, who was working and finishing school. Even as a child, I knew that I was called to preach; and because Grandmother was a preacher, she naturally spent additional time with me.

Her "training" mainly involved prayer and reading God's Word, the Bible. When we had family prayer, my sister and I were not allowed to just sit and listen; and we were certainly not allowed to watch television or color in coloring books when the adults prayed, either!

When it was time to pray, we had to kneel down just as they did. We came from a background where many people felt they weren't really praying if they were not on their knees. Priscilla and I weren't expected to pray the entire time our mother and grandmother prayed, because their prayer times were, on occasion, hours long.

We were, however, instructed to pray as much as we could. Our mother and grandmother understood the limits of our attention spans and physical stamina, and they encouraged us to pray to that point and then just beyond it to build our endurance in prayer. In that way, they trained us to be able to enter into a long period of prayer when we sensed God calling us to do that.

Naturally, we prayed in English, but we also prayed in tongues. The Bible mentions this as a heavenly prayer language, given by God to Christian believers. Most of the time, we do not know exactly what we are praying when we pray in tongues, but the Holy Spirit of God prays through us just what is needed. The apostle Paul mentions the importance of praying in both our human language and in the "unknown" language of tongues in First Corinthians 14:15:

...what shall I do? I will do both. I will pray in unknown tongues and also in ordinary language that everyone understands (TLB).

We also read our Bibles daily at home. It was simply a part of our lifestyle. In some families, the children might be expected to make their beds, fold their own laundry, or care for the pets; in our family, Priscilla and I were expected to read four chapters of the Bible a day, so that we could read it through in a year. This was an assigned "chore," in a sense, but it certainly was not a grinding, unpleasant burden to my sister and me. It was just what we did as a family—how we lived.

My family and I also memorized Scriptures at home as well as at Sunday school. In the mornings, as we ate breakfast or headed out the door to school, Mother or Grandmother—whoever was getting us off to school that day—would ask us what we were memorizing. Sometimes, my sister and I memorized three or four verses during a week.

In hearing me relate these experiences, or after reading about them in my books, some people have received the wrong impression about my upbringing.

A few have said, "Boy! You sure had a tough childhood!"

No, I didn't have a "tough childhood." We lived under a kind of divine discipline that grew out of the love and compassion of my mother and grandmother—and the Spirit of the Lord. The spirit of rebellion that permeates the world never had a chance to take hold of us. Rebellion was simply not allowed in our home.

After my parents' divorce, even more prayer began to take place in our home. And, yes, there were some problems and hurts that I did have to work through because of the divorce. However, as I have talked to and read about many other children of broken homes, I realize that my sister and I came through quite well—and it was *because* of the prayer and emphasis of the Word as we grew up.

Often, God's Word working in our hearts broke feelings of rejection and self-pity that otherwise might have set up what the Bible calls *"strongholds"* (see 2 Cor. 10:4). These strongholds can gain a grip on a life that will cause untold suffering and destruction. Many mornings, as I boarded the school bus, I prayed under my breath or whispered verses of Scripture.

There were times, of course, when I was filled with sorrow that I did not have a dad with whom I could do the things that all boys like to do. Other children would ask me about my dad, which increased my sadness. I found myself wanting to cry, "Where is my dad? Where is he when I need him?"

And suddenly, I would remember my mother and grandmother teaching me, "You may not have a natural father living with you every day, but you do have a heavenly Father who is with you each day. He will be your Dad, if you let Him."

It was at one of those moments, remembering their words, that I had a revelation of a great truth. The seed they had planted inside me began to grow, and I knew beyond any doubt that knowing my heavenly Father was the most important reality in my life.

It was wonderful to have the kind of relationship with God that we had at home. It certainly affected how I acted at school! Because of the strong principles from God's Word that had been placed inside me by prayer, Bible reading, and my mother's and grandmother's teaching, I found I just couldn't use certain words or do some of the things other kids did. Especially during my teenage years, I was, in a sense, "out of step" with my peers; I realize now that it was they who were out of step—with God.

Mother and Grandmother taught me not to lie, or to steal, or to covet. The Ten Commandments really were our way of life. When other children made fun of us and we came home upset, we were told, "Truth outlives a life."

Priscilla and I were not unique in receiving some persecution for the way we lived. The problem of peer pressure exists for Christian teenagers in any situation or generation. We were able to handle it without bending or breaking because of the love and respect we had for our mother and grandmother—and for Jesus.

Respect for Adults

One of the most valuable abilities that was developed in my sister and me was to honor our elders, especially older men and women in the ministry. Today, when I see how many children are allowed to act disrespectfully toward their parents and other adults, I think of the story of the turtle and the hare. You probably heard this story as a child.

A turtle and a hare set out to run a race. The hare, symbolizing a lie, seems to be winning. Whereas, the turtle, representing the truth, looks as if he won't even finish. Everyone pays attention to the lie as it speeds on. But the hare is overconfident and decides to take a nap, thinking he has already won the race. Yet while he sleeps, the turtle overtakes him and crosses the finish line to win the race.

In the same way, in the past 15 years, when rumors have run rampant concerning nearly every well-known ministry and minister, I've thought of that principle. People may say this thing or that, but the truth really will "outlive a life."

Likewise, the truth of honoring one's elders, particularly those "elder statesmen" of the faith, will add to your knowledge and spiritual wisdom. There is much we can learn from those who have gone before us, just as I learned from my grandmother's long experience in the ministry.

I actually come from a long line of preachers; my grandmother learned from her ancestors and passed that knowledge along to me. For several generations, there have been ministers of the Gospel in my family. There were Methodist circuit riders, preachers in various denominations, and my grandfather and grandmother, the first Pentecostal preachers in our family lineage.

The Bible Talks about Visions

Some of the questions that naturally come to mind when people hear of visions or going to Heaven are: "Is this for today?" "Do people really have visions?" "How can I know if these things are from God or not?"

We have an authority to which we can go concerning all spiritual activity—it is the Bible.

On the Day of Pentecost, 40 days after Jesus returned to Heaven following His resurrection from the dead, the apostle Peter quoted a prophecy given hundreds of years earlier by the prophet Joel. Peter said that this prophecy was now to be fulfilled. The "last days" referred to by Joel and Peter actually began on the Day of Pentecost, and continue to this day. In Acts 2:16-18, Peter proclaims:

> *...this is what was spoken by the prophet Joel: "In the last days, God says, I will pour out My Spirit on all people. Your sons and daughters will prophesy, your young men will see visions, your old men will dream dreams. Even*

*on My servants, both men and women, I will pour out
My Spirit in those days, and they will prophesy"* (NIV).

You can see in this Scripture passage several characteristics
that the prophet Joel identified with the "last days"—days in
which we are now living:

- God will pour His Spirit out on all *flesh*, meaning
  that every person will come into contact with God's
  power in some way, and then be faced with how they
  will handle it and respond to the person of Jesus.

- A surge of God's supernatural power will come on
  both men *and* women, young *and* old, and even on
  the very lowliest. This includes whether you have
  an education or not, whether you have certain natural gifts or not. God wants to show Himself mighty
  through *everyone*.

- People, even young ones, will see visions, have supernatural dreams, and prophesy.

Not only does the Bible promise that people will see visions,
but it is filled with the testimonies of those who have had visions
themselves. In Isaiah 6:1, the prophet Isaiah saw the Lord sitting upon a throne, high and lifted up. The prophets Ezekiel,
Jeremiah, and Zechariah, who spoke God's Word to His exiled
children, each had several visions. In Second Kings 2:11, Eli-
sha literally saw the older prophet Elijah taken up bodily into
Heaven by a chariot of fire.

The apostle John, while he was in exile upon the Island of
Patmos, saw a number of spiritual visions, which have been
recorded for us in the Book of Revelation. In Acts 10:9-16,
the apostle Peter fell into a trance and had a vision of clean
and unclean beasts. This vision came to him three times, and
the Lord gave him the interpretation of it—both the Jews (the

"clean") and the Gentiles (the *"unclean")* were included in God's plan of salvation through His Son.

I believe that as time moves toward the return of Jesus, we'll see more and more dreams, visions, and other works of the Holy Spirit. It will become even more important to know God's Word concerning these supernatural manifestations as well as have the discernment by the Holy Spirit as to what is truly of God. The Bible speaks of the devil or satan, who always tries to produce a counterfeit of what God does. When he sees the Holy Spirit moving in a certain way, he comes up with a similar move. Much of what is called "New Age" is nothing more than satan's imitation of God's signs, wonders, and miracles.

There are four types of visions—five actually, if you count what could be called a "false" vision.[1] The first type is referred to as an *open* vision. During this vision, a person's human senses are not suspended, but rather they see directly into the supernatural world. God has literally opened their eyes and ears to the world of the spirit.

An example of this is found in Revelation 4:1-2, where John had his vision on the Island of Patmos:

> *After this I looked, and there before me was a door standing open in heaven. And the voice I had first heard speaking to me like a trumpet said, "Come up here, and I will show you what must take place after this." At once I was in the Spirit, and there before me was a throne in heaven with someone sitting on it* (NIV).

Different from the open vision is the trance vision. In this type of vision, the human senses are suspended, but the person does see into the supernatural world. The apostle Peter experienced this when he had a vision when praying on a roof, in Acts 10:9-10:

*About noon the following day as they were on their jour-
ney and approaching the city, Peter went up on the roof
to pray. He became hungry and wanted something to
eat, and while the meal was being prepared, he fell into
a trance* (NIV).

Peter then saw Heaven opened up and what appeared to
be a large sheet lowered to earth, filled with all kinds of animals, reptiles, and birds. He heard a voice tell him to eat what
was in there. Peter, an observant Jew, replied that he had never
eaten anything impure or unclean. The voice told him never to
call impure what God has made clean. This trance vision was
repeated two more times. Ultimately, Peter realized that salvation through Jesus Christ was not merely for the Jews (who could
be considered "clean" before God because of their covenant with
Him), but it was also for the Gentiles, who had always been considered "unclean."

A third type of vision is the *inward* vision. This vision is often
compared to a dream. The person experiencing it does not see
into the supernatural world, but receives revelation within himself, in his mind. In Daniel 2:28, the prophet Daniel refers to this
as he replies to King Nebuchadnezzar about the king's disturb-
ing dream:

*...there is a God in heaven who reveals mysteries. He has
shown King Nebuchadnezzar what will happen in days
to come. Your dream and the visions that passed through
your mind as you lay on your bed are these* (NIV).

A final type of vision is frequently referred to as a *night* vision
or *dream.* This is mentioned in the story of Mary and Joseph in
Matthew 1:20. Joseph had been pledged to Mary, but she was
now to have a child. Consequently, Joseph planned to separate
from her privately to share her disgrace, when,

After he had considered this, an angel of the Lord appeared to him in a dream and said, "Joseph son of David, do not be afraid to take Mary home as your wife, because what is conceived in her is from the Holy Spirit" (NIV).

These night visions are not just human dreams; they are sent from God and have a supernatural component to them. They don't deal with simple earthly events or human desires, but with God's great plans that He wishes to reveal. Indeed, visions, dreams, and signs that are *from God* always point to Jesus and what He did to redeem mankind. They make His name great rather than lifting up a person. They never offer a *different* path to God, but rather direct men to Jesus, whom John 14:6 tells us is *"the way, the truth, and the life."* They are filled with what is pure, good, true, and holy; furthermore, they never instruct us to violate the commandments and laws of God.

As I have traveled around the world in the past two decades and studied Church history, it has become apparent to me that more and more Christians are experiencing the fulfillment of Joel's prophecy. Many believers tell of dreams and visions about Heaven or hell in books and publications such as *Guidepost* magazine and the Full Gospel Business Men's Fellowship International's monthly publication, *Voice.* Some men of our day report having had more than one vision.[2]

God's Word goes into detail concerning visions and supernatural dreams, making it clear that they are for today; the testimony of many bears this out. Men and women, throughout history and into the present, have received visions from God, and there are more to come. Yet, there is no way you can *earn* a vision or have one simply because you choose to have it. I know that nearly every Christian would like to see Jesus or have a preview of Heaven. There seems to be no set criteria for these experiences except the sovereign will of God. He alone determines who will have them.

Much so-called "New Age" teaching, I have noticed, seems to emphasize the power of our own choice in having visions, dreams, and supernatural experiences whenever we want, "on demand." This, however, is wrong; it is not up to us to decide to have a *supernatural experience* whenever we want. If we try to make something happen, we may experience something supernatural, but it will not be from God. It comes from satan to deceive. Only God decides when and if we will have visions and dreams—we don't.

My primary belief remains that God's will alone is involved in selecting people for these experiences. I also know it's not because He favors those selected, but I believe their visions, dreams, and experiences are meant to help further God's plan on earth in some particular way. Ultimately, I feel He does these things to establish His will and His Kingdom on earth, rather than merely for our benefit or enjoyment. He sends visions for His purposes, by His will.

Although I had this vision of Heaven at age eight, I didn't share it with people until my late teens. The Lord began to speak to me while I was in high school and said that I was to begin telling what He had shown and told me when I was little. He said, "I want you to put this into a book, and I will cause it to go around the earth. It will win more souls than you will in person in your life and ministry."

And I have done exactly that. I have written this story, and when God impresses it upon me, I retell it for the purpose of winning people to Christ. I am also able to comfort those who have lost a family member or a Christian close to them, with the reality of Heaven.

As of this writing, there are more than one million copies of the story of my visit to Heaven in print in many languages.

Chapter Two

A Visit to Heaven

I WAS EIGHT YEARS OLD that summer of 1974 when I came indoors one day around noon. I had been playing a game of baseball outside with my friends, but now it was time to read my four chapters of the Bible. (I knew I'd be quizzed later on it.) As I have said, reading the Bible was simply a part of our family life— a part that I wasn't allowed to ignore. That day's reading was in the Gospel of John. My goal was to quickly finish my reading so I could return outside to the baseball game; I certainly wasn't looking for any deep revelation!

I sat down on the side of my bed and then laid my head back on the pillow, with my *Children's Living Bible* propped up on my chest so I could read it. *Suddenly—without any warning—the bed, my room, and even my body disappeared!*

As this happened, the first thing I felt was an energy or presence, which I now know was the anointing and presence of God. Of course, as an eight year old, I wasn't able to identify it that way. I felt myself being pulled through the roof of my house at a high rate of speed. As I moved over the earth, I began to see the oceans as if from a distance, and moving farther through space, I saw the lights in the heavens.

I did not realize it at the time, but what I was experiencing is mentioned in the Bible. The apostle Paul mentions being *"caught up to the third heaven"* in Second Corinthians 12:2. Today, most Bible scholars agree that the earth's natural atmosphere is the first heaven, and the second heaven is that unseen realm of the spirit—just as real as the natural world, but invisible unless God opens our eyes to it. It is considered to be the place where satan and his demons have lived since being cast out of the third Heaven.

The third Heaven is where God dwells, and due to my experience there, I refer to it as a "planet" called Heaven. It produces the feeling of a geographical location, a definite place at the top of the universe, from which all else proceeds. Scientists tell us that the universe is continuing to expand outwardly, and that seems to fit with what I have seen and experienced.

Of course, as an eight-year-old boy, I didn't perceive it quite that way. And I now tell this experience from the perspective of the eight-year-old I was then. As an adult, I have questions today that didn't even enter my mind at that time, and I have a different understanding of what I saw. At the age of eight, however, I simply accepted the experience without analyzing it a great deal.

One of the Gates

That afternoon, all I knew was that I was flying through the heavens at an incredible rate of speed. In a matter of a few moments, I landed on a flat space no larger than the average living room floor, outside an enormous gate, the biggest I had ever seen—or have ever seen since. It was very tall and wide and bore no cut or blemish. In fact, it was made of one solid pearl, immense, glossy, and glowing white. The edges of the gate were carved with a design. And it had a presence to it—its own glow and its own life.

I remember as a little boy looking at this gate and trying to figure out what in the world had happened! I shook myself to see if I was dreaming because it all had happened so fast. I then realized the gate was real when I reached out my hand and touched it. As I did so, I heard these words: "This is one of the gates."

I turned around to see who had spoken to me, and *there stood Jesus Christ.* All the glory that was about Him began to move toward me, and it came upon me. I recognized Him immediately, although He did not look like any of the pictures I had ever seen painted of Him. This much I can say: When you are faced with the presence of Jesus, you have no doubt who He is.

I Beheld Him

Since that moment when I came face to face with Him, people have asked me repeatedly what He looks like. This is harder to answer than it might seem. In my experience, those who have seen Him are so overwhelmed by His presence that His appearance is secondary. You become so caught up in *who* He is that your mind doesn't fully retain the details of what He looks like.

But I remember that He appeared to me to be somewhere around 5'11" to 6'1" tall and muscular—the perfect man. I saw no scars or signs of His crucifixion. They may have been there, but I did not see them. The way He looked, talked, and moved seemed the epitome of perfection and wholeness. He is God, and I sensed that. His skin was olive-toned, and He had a beard. His hair came almost to His shoulders and appeared to be sandy-brown.

Over the years, people have come to me and said, "But His hair is dark!" Perhaps they think of Him that way due to medieval and Byzantine paintings in which His hair is often black or because He was a Jew. They may be right. Perhaps His hair looked lighter to me because of the light of His presence or His glory that surrounded Him. I can only relate it the way I saw it at the time, and it is still as clear to me as if I had seen Him today.

Furthermore, the only place the New Testament describes details of His appearance is in Revelation 1:14, where the apostle John saw His hair, *"white like wool, as white as snow."* The Bible is fairly silent, for good reason I believe, about His physical appearance. What He "looks" like is not the central issue; knowing Him and experiencing the reality of His presence is. I believe the Lord did not want us to become so caught up in His physical appearance that we would miss the spiritual reality of knowing Him personally. In the same way that we know that we are far more than our height, or hair or skin color, or the shape of our features, so He is far more than His appearance!

And the glory of that presence engulfed me. I buckled to my knees, and tears began to stream from my eyes, running down my face. I could not have stopped them if I had tried. They were not provoked by any human emotion such as sadness or excitement, but by His very presence. When He spoke to me, it was as if arrows of faith propelled by love shot into me and exploded inside. My only reaction was to weep.

Then He spoke again, "I want to give you a tour through Heaven, this place I have made for all who believe, because *I love you so much.*"

And He does not love me anymore than He does you!

Acts 10:34 reveals that God is not a respecter of persons; the measure that He loves one is the same measure with which He loves all. As He said this to me, tears began to pour down my face again. His presence is so tender that your joy cannot express itself in any other way.

Then Jesus said, "Now, no more tears, but a face full of joy would make me glad." And then He laughed, and I did, too.

He came over to me, picked me up, and dried my face. There are no human words to adequately describe either Jesus or Heaven. The people who have seen Him or who have been to Heaven can express only what they have seen in terms of what they know on earth, and that is a poor picture indeed compared to the real thing.

Life in Heaven

Jesus escorted me through that huge gate. He didn't ask anyone to open it, and He pushed no button; it simply opened up and we walked through to the inside of Heaven.

As I entered Heaven, the first thing I saw was a street, and it was made of gold. As I continued to walk through Heaven, I saw that all the streets looked as if they were literally made of pure gold. Even the curbs were made of gold. In some places the streets looked just like the gold we have on earth, which is how I recognized what it was. Yet, in other parts, the streets were transparent, and the gold looked as clear as crystal.

I thought to myself, If this is Heaven, then these are gold streets I'm standing on. And with that, I raced for the curb.

From a distance, I saw that Jesus had continued to walk ahead. He then turned to say something to me, but I had moved. Looking over at me, He inquired, "What are you doing over there?"

I stood on the grass alongside the curb with both my eyes and my mouth wide open in surprise. I answered Him with two words: "Golden streets!" At that, Jesus laughed and laughed. He has a wonderful laugh that comes from deep within, similar to what we call a "belly laugh." I thought He would never stop. Then He said, "Come over here."

I replied, "No. Those streets are gold. I can't walk on them!" The only gold I had ever seen was in rings on people's fingers, which I knew was valuable and very expensive. But Jesus beckoned me. "Come on," He said and kept laughing as He walked over to where I was and led me back onto the street. I would come to realize that the way we look at wood here on earth is the way Heaven looks at gold—useful and beautiful, but nothing out of the ordinary nor impossible to possess.

"These streets were made for those who have accepted Me into their hearts. They are made for My younger brothers and sisters. You are one of My younger brothers, so enjoy them." Jesus spoke to me on my eight-year-old level.

Along the curbs, the grass was a green that I cannot express, except to say it was the original essence and very fullness of that color. In fact, all the colors there were of such a nature that the colors here on earth seem faded in comparison to the vibrancy of Heaven. The curbs were also lined with flowers in all the colors of the rainbow, and they hummed.

No, they weren't little Walt Disney flowers with tiny faces humming little songs! A "hum" emanated from them as they vibrated and surged with the life of God that fills Heaven. While I was looking at them, I noticed a woman coming down the street, and she practically bounced as she went along. This is because the atmosphere in Heaven has no resistance in it. There's "no sweat" to our existence in Heaven. The closest thing that people here on earth can come to this experience is in the spirit of prayer in the spiritual realm, where they get to a place that is carefree, where the pressures of life neither control nor dominate them. There is no devil and no temptation there but a light, free, and joyful atmosphere. I found no sense of hurry in Heaven.

As we walked along, I became aware that the atmosphere of Heaven is wonderful because the fruit of the Holy Spirit energizes it. The very breezes are filled with the presence of God. Often on earth, in the supernatural presence of the Holy Spirit, there is a feeling of inner warmth, of being wrapped in a blanket of God's love. That is the way Heaven felt, only more so.

Jesus and I passed towns, buildings, and little offices. These buildings were used for whatever "business" or interaction that takes place in Heaven. I saw people coming and going, and they all were smiling. Some sang songs I recognized from earth, while others sang heavenly songs I had never heard. Many carried little bundles, and some carried books.

While I don't believe there is an exchange of money in Heaven, there were people going in and out of those buildings to acquire things. I saw a woman walk into one place with a bundle of some type of goods and later walk out with a book.

There are books in Heaven! In Revelation 21:27, the Bible mentions the Lamb's book of life, and there are others, too. There are books and songs in Heaven that are intended for our knowledge and enjoyment in praising God on earth, while others are designed to give not just academic knowledge, but an understanding of the times and seasons of God's plan on earth so people may cooperate with His present-day workings. These books are intended to motivate mankind and bring an impartation of God's very life to those on earth.

There is, however, a price to be paid to bring these books and songs from Heaven to earth for the benefit of the Body of Christ. It is the price of walking in the Spirit—being led by God's Spirit rather than submitting to those desires of ours that oppose Him. You pay this price by spending much time in prayer and loving God's Word more than earthly pleasures, knowledge, and entertainment. The men and women who would bring these books and songs from Heaven must be able to resist both the flattering popularity that might come and the rejection by those who won't understand.

Mansions Prepared for Us

As we walked on through this section of Heaven, which was really like a small town, I saw street signs. We came to one street, the name of which I cannot remember, and we turned right.

We walked up what looked like an unpaved dirt path. Being a small boy, I did what small boys everywhere enjoy doing—I tried to kick up the dirt and make little dust clouds as I walked along. But the path stayed where it belonged! (Whenever I tell this part, the women in the congregation always applaud—they won't have to dust their furniture in Heaven!)

As we continued up the path, I saw a gigantic house above the trees. Even now, as a grown man remembering that house, I know it was a mansion, and that it didn't simply look that way because I was a little boy. While I was in Heaven, I saw different kinds of mansions or homes. They all are not the same size, but each seems to fit the desires of the ones who live in them; each one has some of the features that the person who dwells there likes. It is as if there are touches both of Heaven and of earth in them.

Jesus talked to me the entire time we walked up the path toward the house. You see, Jesus is a person. You can talk to Him about everyday issues, and He'll answer you on your level and according to your understanding, just as He did with me that day in Heaven. He is not only a member of the Godhead who rules and reigns, but He is our *friend,* too. And you don't have to make a visit to Heaven to talk to Him, either! He is here with us on earth, and He has told us in Hebrews 13:5 that He will *never* leave us nor forsake us.

It's important for us to remember that the members of the Trinity—God the Father, Jesus the Son, and the Holy Spirit—have emotions. Likewise, we have emotions because we were created in God's image. However, unlike us, the members of the Godhead aren't "ruled" by their emotions. God, Jesus, and the Holy Spirit always do what is right regardless of emotion. In the same way, while we have emotions to enjoy and to give depth and a unique flavor to our personalities, we need to rule over our own emotions and not allow them to dominate our lives and decisions.

The love of Jesus permeated everything He said and did with me during my visit. I will never forget the revelations I received of what love really is. When we arrived at the door of this mansion, Jesus walked up and knocked on it—a part of His love, being considerate of other people's feelings, time, and privacy. And all the people I met in Heaven were polite.

Jesus and I waited for what seemed like a period of about three minutes, and then He knocked again. Finally, a man opened the door, leaned his head out, and spoke to us. I did not see anyone "floating" through the walls. In fact, the entire time I was in Heaven, I saw no one float anywhere at all. Everyone walked just as we do here on earth!

The man addressed us and said, "How are *You* doing, Jesus? And how are you doing, Roberts?" I almost took off running! That man knew my name, and then pronounced it correctly, with the "s" on the end!

I remember thinking, *How does he know my name? No one but Jesus knows my name up here.* However, to my surprise, I found that everyone who spoke with us knew my name and also knew that I was a visitor. In addition, the conversations were just as they are on earth—people asked questions, answered them, and carried on discussions.

I looked up at the man in shock, but answered him courteously as I had been taught, "Well, I'm doing okay!" He then invited us inside; Jesus and I walked in and sat down in what I would call a living room or den area. The furniture there is different from that on earth in one very important respect—it is as if comfort "lives" in the furniture of Heaven. Earthly furniture becomes uncomfortable after you sit on it for a while, and you find yourself squirming and shifting periodically. In Heaven, comfort finds you. I sat down on a black velvet couch, and comfort reached up and "cuddled" me. I was so comfortable I never had to move once.

The man spoke with Jesus about what we would call revival. I realized that the inhabitants of Heaven have knowledge of events here on earth—not so much political events as what is going on spiritually, such as the movements of God, of the enemy, and of human beings. The man also talked about his family on earth and his concerns for them, again confirming to me that in Heaven people understand what is happening in their physical and spiritual families' lives on earth. If you have family members who have gone to Heaven, they are aware of what is happening in your life and how you are doing.

After we finished talking, the man took us through the house. It can be described only as total perfection. The windows had curtains over them. The walls were decorated with paintings that reminded me of earth's modern art, except they were better.

I saw photographs of the man's family members, and there were plants everywhere. In addition, the mansion was filled with beautiful furniture and luxuries. There were some things, however, that I did not recognize.

Each mansion was suited to the person who lived there, for every child of God has his or her own mansion in Heaven, according to John 14:2. I had the impression that to some degree, your mansion or home there contains what you like and enjoy. This particular one had different rooms, such as the dining room, living room, kitchen, den, and so forth. I'm sure that there were bedrooms, but I did not go upstairs.

The man gave me a large fruit to eat that looked somewhat like an apple, and it was delicious. Afterward, we said good-bye and left through the back door. I cannot begin to tell you why we left that way instead of the front door, but that is the way we went out. There were other people in the house, and they hugged and kissed both of us before we left.

I realize that the idea of eating in Heaven is something many people have a problem believing. The Bible, however, mentions the marriage supper of the Lamb in Revelation 19:9; and in Revelation 22:2, John writes of the tree of life that is in Heaven, bearing 12 kinds of fruit. In addition, John 21:9-14 tells us that Jesus ate fish and bread with the disciples after He was resurrected and had a transfigured body—the kind we will have in Heaven.

Every person I saw looked to be in perfect condition and in the prime of life. They all appeared as if they were in their 30s.

Perhaps this is because the Bible says we shall be like Him, and that was His age when He was resurrected and taken back to Heaven. All the people I saw were friendly and very comfortable with Jesus. They were reverent toward Him, but interacted frequently and easily with Him. You will find that you are perfectly comfortable around Jesus. He is the easiest person to whom you can relate!

The people in Heaven wore white robes, which was the most important item of their dress; it represents the right standing with God that Jesus paid for with His blood. These robes seemed to radiate from within. Some wore different colored sashes, and still others were adorned with jewelry. No one wore crowns, however; I believe that occurrence is still to come.

Children in Heaven

While I was in Heaven, I saw no children. Yet somehow I knew there were children there; they were in another part, which I did not see. I saw only a portion of Heaven, not all of it. Others, however, who have seen or visited Heaven have observed children there.

Earlier in this century, Rebecca Springer lay very ill, near death in Canada. She had a vision of Heaven and saw her niece, Mae, there. As she and Mae walked through Heaven together, they saw little children and adults floating and swimming upon a lake that was as smooth as glass. Later in the vision, she saw a young girl she had known on earth, Mary Bates, who told Rebecca how much she wished her own heartbroken mother could see her there in Heaven and be comforted. Mary's desire was that her mother would understand that her daughter was not lost to her, but would be waiting for her when she, too, joined God's saints, that is, believers in Christ.

Perhaps the most moving part of Rebecca's vision was seeing Jesus sitting beneath a flowering tree on the shore of the lake, surrounded by a dozen children of all ages. Some sat at His feet or leaned upon His knees and His shoulders. One tiny girl sat upon His lap, her hands filled with flowers, as Jesus talked with them. Their faces shone with ecstasy as He told them a story and asked them questions. Rebecca's vision confirms that Jesus has a special, tender love for those little ones of His in Heaven.[3]

In 1988, evangelist Jesse Duplantis was taken up into Heaven. While he was there, he saw a multitude of small children, singing and praising God as they played little harps. When he asked the angel who had brought him there who they were, he was told they were the children the earth did not want. As Duplantis watched these children, who appeared to be from three to ten years old, he realized that they were children who had been lost to abortion. The angel explained to him that these children longed to see their mothers come to Heaven and be reunited with them.[4]

The children continued to play their beautiful music when Jesus appeared to them. His hands reached out to them as they played their harps and sang praises to Him. They hugged Him and looked up at Him in adoration. He responded by saying, *"Suffer the little children to come unto me...for of such is the kingdom of God"* (Mark 10:14b).

Norvel Hayes, a successful Christian businessman from Tennessee, also received a vision from the Lord that concerned children in Heaven. In this vision, which he experienced almost 30 years ago, he saw a large, gray, mansion-like building. The Lord permitted him to go into the many rooms there, and he saw furniture designed just for little children—little chairs and tables and such. It was as if the entire mansion had been prepared as a home for children. As he walked outside the building, he saw beautiful flowers filled with the life of God and brilliant green grass. The presence of God in the air was so strong; every time he breathed, he experienced a divine sensation of goodness and beauty.

After his vision, he told everyone he met who had lost a young child to sickness or to an accident, "If you could see where your child lives today, you would never wish for him or her to come back! God has made a special place in Heaven just for children."

Fourteen years later in Florida, as his driver pulled out on the highway to go to the Gainesville airport, the Spirit of the Lord came upon Norvel Hayes so strongly that he had to hold on to the door. As he wept in God's presence, everything earthly disappeared, and God gave him another vision. He saw little children all around him, trying to reach him, holding up their hands. These children were needy, crying, "Help me!" And the vision ended.

About a month later, while attending a camp meeting in Springfield, Missouri, a message was given in tongues at the end of the service, and the interpretation of it was meant personally for Norvel Hayes. God reminded him that He had not forgotten about the little children.

"I am going to require you to get a building for Me, to help save little children." Hayes bought a repossessed mansion-like building with seven bathrooms and twelve bedrooms, which became a home for unwed mothers. An untold number of children have been saved through this ministry, born out of that vision. His vision of Heaven has brought comfort to parents who have aborted children or lost them at a young age, and it has also given birth to a ministry devoted to helping children here on earth.

While there are adults and children in Heaven, I found that each person's age is reckoned according to his or her spiritual maturity, not their physical maturity on earth. When you get to Heaven, your age will be what you are spiritually in the hidden man of the heart.

Animals in Heaven

Jesus and I continued walking, and as we crossed some hills, I noticed other things. I saw all kinds of animals, every kind you can think of, from A to Z. Often, people have questioned the subject of animals in Heaven, but if you think about it, why should there not be animals in Heaven? The Bible talks about horses in Heaven—and why would God have only one kind of animal? The most well-known reference, of course, is regarding Jesus returning to earth on a white horse, found in Revelation 19:11. When the prophet Elijah was taken up into Heaven, a fiery horse and chariot were sent down after him.

While I was in Heaven, I saw a dog, a baby goat, and a lion of great strength. There were birds singing in the trees, all sizes of birds, and they seemed to be singing the same song. And I could understand what they were singing—there was no "communication gap." When they stopped singing, it seemed as if they began to talk among themselves.

I receive letters from people, asking if their pets will be in Heaven? I don't know the answer to that. You'll have to wait and see. I will say this—if everyone's dog, cat, parakeet, ferret, hamster, and gerbil show up, we're going to have a *lot* of animals in Heaven!

There were other animals I saw at a distance, but I could not identify them. They neither ran from people nor tried to attack them. All were calm and peaceful, because *fear cannot be found in Heaven.* God's presence is so strong that there is no confusion, doubt, sickness, or worry there.

I noticed the trees as we passed. The leaves swayed back and forth, dancing and praising. You would have thought a great wind was blowing through the land. The grass was very soft and yet after we passed over it, the blades sprang back into perfect alignment, immediately erasing any footprints.

I think many men will be happy to know that you never have to mow the lawn in Heaven! The grass is always the same length. After a leaf falls from a tree, it disappears. There is never any rotten fruit on a tree because death and decay cannot exist in Heaven. There is not one thing wrong there and not one problem to be found.

Of course, no death is found there, because the source of life is there. The goodness of God abounds in Heaven.

Chapter Three

MULTITUDES OF ANGELS

JESUS AND I BECAME FRIENDS as He continued to take me on a tour of Heaven. I was very comfortable with Him and not a bit nervous about what I said or did. When I looked down at myself, I discovered that I was dressed just as all the other people we met. All the saints whom I saw were dressed in white robes.

But it was not only people I saw in Heaven; it was also filled with angels. Sometimes paintings and other artwork give us a misleading impression of angels, that they are chubby, smiling, naked babies floating through the air playing harps. They are not like that at all! The angels I saw in Heaven were tall and strong; they appeared to be from six to eight feet tall and were dressed according to their position.

Some angels I saw did not have wings—but others did. When those wings moved, a musical sound was created, the like of which we have been unable to duplicate on earth. Many times, I have met older people in Christian circles who say they have heard angels sing—it may have been the sound of those wings moving, creating the melody of Heaven. When I stood on the streets of Heaven talking to people, angels would walk up to us, their wings would move, and I would hear the sound.

I noticed that angels acted differently in Jesus' presence than people did. Where people were reverent, but talkative and friendly with Jesus, the angels were almost silent, respectful, and reserved in His presence. I believe this is due to the fundamental difference between angels and humans.

Not all angels are the same; the Bible classifies them into several groups. Among these are the cherubim, the seraphim, the archangel, and the common angel. There are also warrior angels and messenger angels and probably many kinds not mentioned in Scripture.

Cherubim are described particularly in the Book of the prophet Ezekiel. Although often portrayed in popular art as fat, romantic babies shooting arrows of "love" at people, their reality is far different. They are often not classed as angels, but as a different order of being. They protected the Garden of Eden with flaming swords after Adam and Eve had been put out of Eden to live on the earth.

Among other characteristics, the cherubim (plural of "cherub") each have four faces and four wings with feet like those of calves. They do not "turn" as they move, but go straight forward. One of their faces is that of a man in front, one like that of a lion on the right side, another like that of an ox on the left side, and the remaining one is like the face of an eagle in back. Two of their wings are joined to each other and the other two cover their body.

Cherubim have an appearance similar to that of burning coals of fire, from which lightning goes forth. They have four hands, in appearance like that of a man. As they moved, Ezekiel heard the noise of a great rushing.

The main function of cherubim in Scripture is that of covering or protecting. Nowhere is this more evident than in Ezekiel 41:18-21, where there are carvings of cherubim placed all around the temple as a sign of being covered with God's protection. In the same way, in Exodus 37:7-9, Moses had been told to make golden replicas of cherubim to shadow or cover the ark of the covenant.

The seraphim are described in Isaiah chapter 6 as having six wings; two cover their faces, two cover their feet, and they fly with the other two. In verse 3, the seraphim stand above the throne of God and cry out to each other, *"Holy, holy, holy, is the Lord of hosts: the whole earth is full of His glory!"* Their purpose is to recognize and proclaim His holiness and His majesty.

In Isaiah 6:1-7, the prophet has a vision of the Lord on His throne, with the seraphim flying about Him, calling out to each other of His holiness. As Isaiah is confronted with his own sinfulness and cries out to God, it is the seraphim that fly to him, bringing a live coal from the altar, and laying it upon his mouth to purge his sin.

At the top of the angelic hierarchy are the chief angels, known as archangels. These angels rule over entire kingdoms. The Bible names three of them: Michael, the prince of Israel, mentioned in Daniel 10:13,21; Gabriel who stands before God and announced the birth of Jesus to His mother, Mary, in Luke 1:26-38; and lucifer, or "light-bearer," the angel who mounted a rebellion against God and was cast down from Heaven with one third of the angels.

Lucifer—The Fallen Angel

Ezekiel 28:14-17 gives us a detailed picture of this prince of angels who was the ruler of earth before his fall:

You were anointed as a guardian cherub, for so I ordained you. You were on the holy mount of God; you walked among the fiery stones. You were blameless in your ways from the day you were created till wickedness was found in you. Through your widespread trade you were filled with violence, and you sinned. So I drove you in disgrace from the mount of God, and I expelled you, O guardian cherub, from among the fiery stones. Your heart became proud on account of your beauty, and you corrupted your wisdom because of your splendor. So I threw you to the earth; I made a spectacle of you before kings (NIV).

It is apparent that lucifer—or satan, as he is now known—had a position of great authority, was tremendously beautiful, and yet sinned against God. Isaiah 14:12-15 sheds more light on his fall:

How you have fallen from heaven, O morning star, son of the dawn! You have been cast down to the earth, you who once laid low the nations! You said in your heart, "I will ascend to heaven; I will raise my throne above the stars of God; I will sit enthroned on the mount of assembly, on the utmost heights of the sacred mountain. I will ascend above the tops of the clouds; I will make myself like the Most High." But you are brought down to the grave, to the depths of the pit (NIV).

Lucifer had decided to rule Heaven in God's place and make himself like God. However, God threw him out of Heaven into the lowest depths! This is an event that has fascinated men throughout the millennia. The Puritan poet, John Milton, is his epic work, *Paradise Lost,* describes God casting lucifer from Heaven, declaring, "Him the Almighty Power hurl'd headlong flaming from th' Ethereal sky with hideous ruin and combustion down to bottomless perdition."[5] Banished forever from Heaven, lucifer, or satan, has become the false "ruler" of earth. Jesus stripped Him of his powers at the cross; all he has left is the power of deception. It is he who deceives people about spiritual reality and tries to impersonate the Holy Spirit and the angels of God. The Bible now refers to him as an angel of light, who appears to radiate with the light of God's revelation, but who is actually false and deceiving.

How can we know which angels are from God? What are the characteristics of divine angels, as opposed to demon spirits?

First, angels are sent from Almighty God. They bring messages of healing and deliverance. They do not speak for themselves, but are always under the authority of God. They are perfectly holy, and they always obey the Word of God. Their entire behavior agrees with the commandments and principles of Scripture.

Angels will never force themselves and their ministry upon you—but demons will. An angel may come with healing power, but you will have to choose to open the door of your heart to it.

In the past ten years, angels have become a popular subject of books, television programs, and even movies. Unfortunately, much of the "information" we find there is simply not true. Humans can never become angels when they die. Angels and men are two separate orders of being. Humans don't become angels, and angels can never turn into humans! And despite the Christmas favorite, *It's a Wonderful Life,* no angel can "earn his wings"! Nothing in Heaven is earned by personal effort—good or bad.

A more recent movie showed one of the archangels—a chief angel of God—coming to earth, where he proceeded to smoke, curse, drink, and chase women. No angel would ever dream of behaving this way, much less doing it and joking about it! In yet another film concerning angels, these ominous beings were dressed in gloomy black, and one finally decided to leave Heaven forever in order to live on earth and engage in a sexual relationship with a woman. Although it was portrayed as a tender love story of sacrifice for another, it is false when it comes to the real character, nature, and behavior of angels.

Many books encourage readers to regularly talk to and have experiences with their own personal angel. While it is true that angels are messengers from God and that we can speak to them, they can never take that first-place position in our lives that belongs only to the Lord Jesus. It cannot be stated too clearly that some of this so-called communication with angels is nothing more than *contact with demon spirits*. We cannot force angels to appear to us or communicate with us—that, too, is left up to the sovereign will of God.

Our Guardian Angels

It is true, however, that each of us is assigned an angel to be our guardian. Every one of us has at least one, and during different seasons and circumstances in our lives, more may be assigned by God to us. Matthew 18:10 reveals:

> *Watch that you don't treat a single one of these childlike believers arrogantly. You realize, don't you, that their personal angels are constantly in touch with my Father in heaven?* (MSG)

Dr. Roy Hicks, in his book *Guardian Angels: How to Activate Their Ministry in Your Life,*[6] recounts a story of a missionary in Panama. This particular missionary had joined with another to travel far back into a country, where the good news of Jesus Christ had not been proclaimed. They knew there would possibly be severe persecution. These two did, however, have a certain amount of success in their outreach and were able to start a church from the meeting they had held.

Returning the next year to encourage the fledgling congregation, the missionaries met a recent convert who indicated a house in the distance, asking if they remembered that they had slept there the year before. When the missionaries responded that they did indeed remember, the new believer explained that at the time, he and others had planned to kill the two while they slept. They were prevented from doing this, he went on to say, by the presence of *two extremely large men guarding the house.*

The two missionaries thanked God for the guardian angels He had sent to protect them!

We often think of guardian angels as protecting little children—and they do; but there is also a guardian angel for every believer. The "little ones" mentioned in Matthew 18 are not only young children, but also Christians of all ages, who are God's children, *His* "little ones."

A Song They Cannot Sing

The angels of God are awe-inspiring beings who bring messages of deliverance to mankind, provide divine protection, and continually proclaim the glory and worthiness of the Godhead. Yet, as wonderful as they are, they do not compare with the love, tenderness, and majesty of Jesus. And, you and I—and all believers here on earth or in Heaven—have one thing even the angels do not have: We have salvation purchased for us by Jesus' death on the cross.

There is an old hymn that tells us that "we sing a song the angels cannot sing." That song is the song of redemption. The angels will never sing it because they cannot be born again. Salvation was made for man; only humans can know His redemption, bought with the blood of Jesus. And unlike the angels, we were not made only to be God's *servants.* All of mankind has been created for the position of greatest dignity as the sons of God and joint-heirs with Jesus Christ.

Chapter Four

LORD, SAVIOR—AND FRIEND

AS JESUS AND I WALKED on, I soon saw a huge building resembling a convention center here on earth. Thousands of people, the saints of God, were streaming inside. The building itself had a glowing circle around it. Two angels met Jesus and me and escorted us down to the second row where two seats were reserved. People greeted us on the way to our seats, and there was not a sad face in the entire place.

You would have thought we were at a family reunion where people had not seen one another in years. They began to hug and kiss each other, saying, "How are you? Glory to God!" It seemed as if they were permeated with an attitude of love—they loved everyone! They didn't care what you looked like or where you were from. They just loved you, and everything they did was motivated by that love.

As soon as we were seated, a holy hush swept over the entire auditorium. I could have heard a pin drop. From the right of the stage, a choir of five to six hundred "praisers" entered, smiling as they walked on stage. These were people, not angels, and they were dressed similarly to a church choir on earth. They wore robes, and everything about their appearance was perfect. Suddenly, they began to sing and from that hushed quiet, those assembled *erupted* into singing and praise. They lost all resemblance to a formal choir from that point!

Their hands went up, their voices lifted in praise songs, and they began to dance. Our praise services on earth could not compare. The congregation joined in, every person singing with all their hearts. They were not ashamed to praise God, either. Everyone in the building lifted their hands, praised God, and leaped up and down in dance. The service seemed to last for about two hours.

No individual led the worship, but everyone moved in unison. In spite of the singing and dancing, everything was done in perfect order—everything. There was no "dead space" or silence. The praise never died down, but instead grew in power and momentum. When I looked over at Jesus, He was smiling broadly and obviously enjoying the service. Then, all of a sudden, the praise ended abruptly, instead of diminishing gradually.

Here on earth, we often let our time of praise die down too soon. We neglect to continue because we have not learned the sacrifice of praise and worship. To really praise God, we need to cross the "line in the spirit" where joy becomes evident in our praise. If we will do that, I believe we will see signs and wonders.

Praise is a substance. I saw all praise ascending out of the mouths of the people as bright, glowing vapors that collected at the top of the building. When the service was complete, the collected praise shot out of the top of the building and went to the throne room of God. I realized that praise and worship are not a routing or merely a preliminary to a message; they are a substance that is created.

In my ministry, I have seen many miracles occur as we have worshiped God, when everyone present was giving his or her all to God. This is the secret—you must not hold back, but give everything you have to God in order to receive everything He has to give you in return. Likewise, those saints I saw in Heaven gave 100 percent to everything they did. They greatly enjoyed the service and said afterward that they could not wait for the next one. Praising God will be a tremendous part of our lives when we get to Heaven.

Jesus asked me, "How did you like the service?"

I replied, "I loved it!"

Tears of Intercession

We left the building, and as we walked along, Jesus began to weep. I was astounded. Jesus the Christ, the Son of God, began to cry! He turned toward me, shedding tears of intercession. Some things are too sacred to repeat, but this one thing He told me I could tell:

"Roberts, I love My people so much that I would go back to earth, preach My three years over again, and die for just one person. If I had not already paid the price for them, and if I thought they wanted to come to Heaven, I would do it all over again.

"I would not have to *know* they would make it. If I just thought they *wanted* to come, I would do it for them, even if they were the greatest sinners of all."

He said repeatedly, "I love My people so much. Why do people not take Me at My word? Do they not know that I have all power in Heaven and on earth to back up what I said? It is so easy. I made it so simple. If people will just take Me at My word, I will do what I said."

Then He wept even more and said, "I do not understand why people say they believe I will do something, but when it does not happen in their time, they begin to doubt My word. If they will just believe and say with confidence that I will do it, I will do it at the correct time."

I knew that Jesus was crying because of our unbelief and lack of faith. Even though I was only eight years old, I knew what unbelief was and how it hurt Him. I made a covenant, an agreement and solemn commitment, with Jesus right then never to doubt His words, and to let God be God. Now, when I am about to think or say something filled with doubt, I remember the tears of intercession that fell from Jesus' eyes, and I rid myself of doubt and unbelief. Unbelief slaps Jesus in the face; it is a rejection of *Him*. He wants us to be filled with faith—strong faith!

The River of Life

Jesus and I continued on together and came to a branch of the river of life. I assume there is only one river in Heaven, although there may be more; I saw only one. The river of life is described in Revelation 22:1 as being crystal bright, flowing from the throne of God and the Lamb. In Revelation 22:17, Jesus says that He gives the pure water from it freely to the thirsty. It purifies you and cleanses you of the contamination of the earth life and gives you strength from its source, that place where God sits and rules as King of the universe.

When Jesus and I walked up to the river of life, we didn't just look at it, but walked into it. It was knee-deep and perfectly clear. Unlike a river on earth, it doesn't just flow around you. It flows *through* you, and you feel a surge of energy come up out of that water and into your being.

Then Jesus did something that is quite personal and extremely precious to me. I love to tell this part of the story.

The Lord Jesus, the Holy Son of God, reached over and dunked me under the water of the river of life.

So I got back up, splashed Him, and we proceeded right there to have a water fight, splashing each other and laughing.

This is not easy for some people to understand, and I have sometimes received the response, "How dare you splash the Lord Jesus in the river of life!" My only answer to this is, "Well, He started it!"

As unexpected as it might be to hear this, or for me to experience it, it meant something really profound to me. Jesus, the King of Glory, the Holy Lamb of God, took time out for little eight-year-old Roberts Liardon to play with him in the river of life. He related to me in a way that I could particularly understand and respond to as an eight-year-old boy.

When my time on earth is done and I return to Heaven forever, I want to put up a historical marker on that spot, which will say: This spot is where Jesus Christ became not only Roberts Liardon's Lord and Savior, but his Friend.

This is holy and very special to me. Jesus is still the rightful Lord of the entire universe. He is the only Savior of mankind. But that day, He became my personal friend. It has been that single experience that has helped me all through my life. When circumstances and the enemy have buffeted me, when I have felt like quitting, it is this one moment that has caught me, picked me up, and kept me on the path God has marked out for me.

If believers here on earth could come to know Him not only as Lord and Savior, but also as friend, how it would transform their lives! In times of temptation, failure, and sin, they would run to Him, instead of away from Him. They would find that He is concerned with the smallest and most intimate areas of their lives and that He longs to help them and make their path clear and straight. They would serve Him with joy in willing response to His love, rather than cower before Him as a taskmaster whose wrath they fear. They would know that He is *for* them and not against them.

After Jesus and I played in the river of life for a while, we got out. It was as if a giant hair dryer then began to blow and dried our clothes instantly. We put on our shoes and departed, and we began to walk past more buildings, seeing other people.

Then we passed something I never expected to see in Heaven and which struck me at the time as the funniest thing I had seen. Yet, when I considered it later, it was one of the most moving and encouraging sights of my Christian walk with God.

Hebrews 12:1 speaks of a "great cloud of witnesses":

> *Therefore, since we are surrounded by such a great cloud of witnesses, let us throw off everything that hinders and the sin that so easily entangles, and let us run with perseverance the race marked out for us* (NIV).

I saw that great cloud of witnesses. *They are aware of what the Church is doing spiritually.* When I am preaching, for example, they are cheering me on, yelling, "Do this...do that...go!" When "halftime" comes, every one of them hits his knees and begins to pray. Halftime is prayer time. Then they get back up and start cheering again.

It is as though we are in a big game, one that is serious and for real—not a game just for fun! And we have some fans who are cheering us on. They are backing us 100 percent saying, "Go! Go get 'em! That's right. Go!"

If we clearly understood the Scripture about there being one family in Heaven and earth, we would hear in our spirits what our family in Heaven is saying. If we could hear that *"cloud of witnesses,"* we would be successful in every area of our lives. To do this, we must enter the realm of the spirit through prayer and time spent with the Lord.

People have asked me from time to time about their own family members who have passed on: "Will I see my cousin when I get to Heaven, and will I know him?" I have been asked if I saw any of my family members who went on before, and I did not. I saw the Lord, angels, and various people. I know who my relatives are, but I did not happen to see them.

I am convinced that even though you *will* recognize your cousin or wife or child when you get to Heaven, you may be surprised to discover that the importance of your *spiritual family* outweighs that of your natural family. While your natural family members in Heaven will always be precious to you, there will be some relationships with the spiritual family in Heaven that will be equally and sometimes more important to you there.

Chapter Five

BLESSINGS THAT HAVEN'T BEEN CLAIMED

THE NEXT SIGHT ON MY tour of Heaven was another building. This one was very large and had a particularly strange appearance to me. I became very curious about this building because lightning flashed into it, and I heard rumblings of thunder from within.

Usually, I asked questions of Jesus in an audible voice, and He answered me audibly. This time, however, I just thought, I wonder what that building is, and His answer came to me immediately.

"It is the throne room of God."

Another unique aspect of this building was the seven rows of flowers in the front. They lined the pathway up to the door. The colors of these flowers changed constantly into all the colors of the rainbow. Every flower, bud, and leaf was uniform in size.

Also, in front of this building were 12 trees—not trees such as that grow on earth, but Heaven's trees. I saw the tree of wisdom that bears the fruit of wisdom, the tree of love that bears the fruit of love, and so forth. Revelation 22:2 tells us about the tree of life and its fruit and leaves:

> *On each side of the river grew Trees of Life, bearing twelve crops of fruit, with a fresh crop each month; the leaves were used for medicine to heal the nations* (TLB).

That is exactly what I saw. I also saw two warrior angels standing in front of the door. Each held a sword, and the blades of these swords were flames of fire. These two angels always stand outside the throne room with their flaming swords fully lit.

The Storehouses of Heaven

We walked a little farther, and *this is perhaps the strangest part of my story.* I saw three storage houses, five to six hundred yards from the throne room of God. They were very long and wide and seemed to be shaped similarly to one of those large chicken houses you see out in the countryside where hundreds of chickens are raised. There may be more of these storehouses, but I saw only three.

We walked into the first one. As Jesus shut the front door behind us, I looked around the interior in shock!

On one side of the building I saw exterior parts of the human body, all different colors, corresponding to different ethnic groups. And on the other side of the building, I saw eyes—green, brown, blue ones—eyes of all colors. It all appeared very normal to me.

I realize people may ask what the biblical basis for this storehouse is. There are no Scriptures supporting it, but neither does it violate the principles of Scripture. As an adult, if I saw that today, I'd have many questions. But at age eight, I simply observed.

This building contained all the parts of the human body that people on earth need, but Christians have not realized these blessings are waiting for them in Heaven. There is no place else in the universe for these parts to go except right here on earth; no one else needs them.

Jesus then began to tell me, and I am paraphrasing Him, that these were the *unclaimed blessings.* He said that this building should not be full, but rather that it should be emptied. I was to go in there with faith and get the needed parts for the people with whom I would come in contact that day.

The unclaimed blessings are there in those storehouses—all the parts of the body that people might need. Hundreds of new eyes, legs, skin, hair, eardrums—they all are there. All you have to do is go in and get what you need by the hand of faith, because it is there!

You do not have to cry and beg God to make the part you need. Just go get it. The doors to the storehouse are never locked. They are always open for those who need to go in. *We should empty those buildings!*

Sometimes when we pray, an angel will leave Heaven to bring us the answer just as the angel did for Daniel, in Daniel 10:12, but will not be able to get through right away. Daniel continued to pray and fast for 21 days until he received his answer. Because of his persistence in prayer, the angel was able to break through demonic hindrances. What would have happened if Daniel had not kept praying and "pressing in" to God for his answer?

If he were like many Christians today, he would have said, "This doesn't work! God didn't answer!" And he would never have received his miracle. In the same way that Daniel did, we must continue to believe God. He has said those storehouses would one day be empty—it's up to us. We need to behold the miraculous in a new way because the closer we come to the end of this age, the greater increase we will see in signs and wonders. See yourself in a position to be one who works miracles on the earth!

Jesus Wants Us Healed and Whole

Because of my visit to Heaven, I never had any doubt that Jesus not only wants His people well and whole, but that healing is available for any who will receive. During my visit, I knew without any doubt that God did not have sickness or disease in Heaven, but rather He had made provision for creative miracles here on earth, where limbs grow back or organs are reformed over a short period of time.

Everything God gives us, has made for us, or provided for us has its source in Him and His heavenly Kingdom. So how could He give us sickness and disease when it is a purely earthly phenomenon, a result of the fall of Adam and Eve? Sickness, disease, lack of anything, and all the other woes of earth come from satan, the father of lies and the cause of death and destruction.

However, I don't base my knowledge of Jesus' provision for healing on my experience in Heaven. I base it on the Word of God. There are many good books available on healing and not enough space in this one to deal with it in detail. But I do want to give two Scriptures that prove healing is ours, for the benefit of those who may not know this or may have been taught otherwise.

But he was pierced for our transgressions, he was crushed for our iniquities; the punishment that brought us peace was upon him, and by his wounds we are healed (Isaiah 53:5 NIV).

This was a prophetic statement made by Isaiah as he looked forward to the time when Jesus would come to earth as the Messiah and go to the cross for mankind.

He himself bore our sins in his body on the tree, so that we might die to sins and live for righteousness; by his wounds you have been healed (1 Peter 2:24 NIV).

The apostle Peter quoted that same passage from Isaiah, but changed the verb. Isaiah looked to the future; Peter used a past-tense verb. Isaiah looked forward to the advent of Jesus who would come *"with healing in his wings"* (Mal. 4:2). Peter however, spoke of our healing as already having been accomplished for us.

Jesus wants us to be physically well for two reasons: He loves us and does not want us to be in pain, and He wants us to be able to do His will in ministry or in our lives without hindrances. Sickness and disease keep your mind on yourself rather than on others; they drain finances that could be used in the Lord's work and give satan that much victory in your life.

I have met many people who have been taught that God uses sickness and disease "to teach us a lesson." That is totally unscriptural. Would you give measles or smallpox to your child to "teach him or her a lesson"? If so, you would be no better than a child abuser. Likewise, God would be considered a child abuser if He disciplined us with sickness and disease.

In Matthew 7:11, Jesus pointed out that if earthly fathers give their children good things, how much more will our Father in Heaven give good things to us who are His children! He asked them if they would give their children a snake if they asked for a fish. And so, why do people think God would do such a thing? Healing is a good thing, and God wants to give it to us.

I did not know all these things when I visited Heaven, but I learned them from God's Word as I grew up. However, I knew after my visit that it is always the will of God to heal everyone who will hear and obey, which under the new covenant means walking in the love of God and your neighbor, and in faith. Jesus said:

> *Listen to Me! You can pray for anything, and if you believe, you have it; it's yours!* (Mark 11:24 TLB)

> *But when he asks, he must believe and not doubt, because he who doubts is like a wave of the sea, blown and tossed by the wind. That man should not think he will receive anything from the Lord* (James 1:6-7 NIV).

Even before my visit to Heaven, as long as I can remember, I have believed that God's Word is true.

After Jesus showed me the throne room of God and the place where all the unclaimed blessings are kept, we walked on a while and were quiet. I was thinking over everything I had seen and was content just to be in the presence of Jesus.

Then Jesus began to tell me what He had called me to do as my life's work on earth.

Chapter Six

JESUS ORDAINED ME TO HIS WORK

JESUS STOPPED, FACED ME, AND took both my hands in one of His, placing His other hand on top of my head. He said to me, "Roberts, I am calling you to a great work. I am ordaining you to a great work. You will have to run like no one else and preach like no one else. You will have to be different from everyone else."

In other words, He was telling me not to copy others, not to try to fit into religious attitudes and patterns, but simply to do and be only what He wanted.

"Hard times will come," He warned me, "but take them as stepping stones, not as stumbling blocks. Go with power and with faith. I will be beside you wherever you go. Go, go, go, go and do as I have done."

The first time Jesus said, "Go," the anointing and the fire of God began to flow from Him into me. It felt as if I were burning.

Now, every time I talk about God, whether it is to one or three thousand, I am set afire all over again, just as Luke 3:16 says:

John answered them all, "I baptize you with water. But one more powerful than I will come, the thongs of whose sandals I am not worthy to untie. He will baptize you with the Holy Spirit and with fire (NIV).

God's people, the Church, need to experience the "fire" of God, which is what burns out all the "chaff," the impurities, in your life. Hebrews 12:29 tells us:

For our God is a consuming fire (NIV).

I cannot tell all that He said to me that day for it is too personal. However, I can say this—if you will let the fire of the Holy Spirit shoot through your being and make you pure, you will be able to walk boldly before God with a clean heart and a clear mind. You will know you can walk into His presence where you belong without being destroyed by His glory.

After praying for me and ordaining me to His work, Jesus took a step backward. I then looked down at the palms of my hands. Their appearance seemed almost as red as blood.

As Jesus stepped back from me, it was as if He pulled down a large screen out of the air. On this screen, He began to show me my past life. Of course, at eight years of age, I did not have much of a past life.

When Jesus began to show me my future ministry and the people who would be saved through it, however, I did not want to miss reaching a single one of them—even if it *did* mean living to be an old man.

He said, "I want you to return to earth, and not be like anyone whom you've ever met or known, and do exactly what

I've called you to do. I've placed inside you the ability and the strength to do it."

The greatest miracle, greater than even raising Lazarus from the dead is the one that occurs when someone is born again—raised from spiritual death and rescued from eternal damnation. In John 3:3, Jesus spoke of this greatest of miracles and the necessity of it for us to enter Heaven:

> *I tell you the truth, no one can see the kingdom of God unless he is born again* (NIV).

Among other passages, the apostle Paul explains what happens to the person who is born again in Second Corinthians 5:17:

> *Therefore, if anyone is in Christ, he is a new creation; the old has gone, the new has come!* (NIV)

As He spoke these things to me, I saw myself preaching in various places. The screen disappeared. Then, I knew it was time to go.

I was turning to leave through the nearest gate when Jesus said, "Roberts!" And I turned back very quickly. There stood Jesus with tears falling down His face and with His hands outstretched to me.

"I love you!"

When He said that, I left Heaven and returned to my earthly home.

Meeting My Angel

On my way back toward earth, I remember meeting my angel, who flew up next to me and introduced himself. "I am the one who is with you. I'm the one who stands with you. I'm the one who assists you. I'm the one who protects you." And he began to list the various services he performs for me.

Then he told me, "I will be with you, even throughout eternity, and I will stand by your side. There will be other angels who will come and go throughout your life, according to the season and the anointings that you carry. There will be different angels, for angels and anointings work together."

And then I was back in my room.

Back on Earth

I was startled, of course, and I lay on my bed wondering about everything I had just experienced. I realized the experience had indeed been real, because the fire of God and the anointing continued to flow in me for several hours after I came back.

My trip to Heaven had been so special that I cherished it close within me for a while. I was not sure that anyone would believe a little boy could be taken to Heaven for a tour with Jesus. Thus, it was nearly eight more years before I ever told anyone about this experience.

I have always sensed that I was a type of forerunner for the young people whom God will use in this generation. In my ministry, I challenge the older people to fulfill God's calling, but I identify with the young people.

My life and ministry, I believe, have become examples of what God can do with you, *if you will pay the price.* The price is total commitment, being totally "sold out," as it were, to the will of God. Part of that price is praying each day and studying God's Word. The price requires putting Jesus before absolutely everything else.

First, you must choose whom you are going to serve. You will have to give up everything you have into God's hands—everything from A to Z and beyond.

Jesus and I are friends. We walk and talk together. When I travel, we get on the plane together. He sits down beside me. He does everything with me.

In the mornings, when I wake, I say, "Good morning, Father. Good morning, Jesus. Good morning, Holy Spirit." We cannot know the Trinity of the Godhead by our feelings, but rather we learn to know them by the Word of God. Our emotions are fickle; they have been influenced by the environment of this world and by its thinking. They are not dependable. But if we will study God's Word, we *will* learn to know God better.

God has a personality. He has emotions. He can be hurt because we have not talked to Him or spent time with Him lately. I have found that He is three things: *light, life,* and *love.* God loves people so much that the love simply boils up out of His being.

All throughout the Bible, men have been friends of God. Abraham is referred to particularly as the friend of God. Daniel talked with God. Likewise, you can be a friend of God. When was the last time you said, "God, I love You"? Perhaps that time is overdue. Jesus wants us to be friends with Him. Many people who are His servants are not His friends; to be His friend requires our obedience.

God wants to know you intimately, and He will meet you more than halfway. All you need to do is sit down and say, "God, I want to talk to You."

Jesus cares about you! If He did not, He would not have died for you. He is concerned about everything that concerns you—your lifestyle, your welfare, your family, everything.

The Holy Spirit wants to do wonderful works on your behalf. He is the One who opens blind eyes and also takes the spiritual blinders off people's eyes. He is the One who reveals the things of God to you. *He is the Trinity's power on earth,* and the One who has come to live inside you. According to Romans 8:11, His is the same power that raised Jesus from the dead. If we could really grasp that, none of us would remain sick.

You and I need to learn how to walk and talk with God in the same way that Enoch did. The Bible tells us in Genesis 5:24 that Enoch walked with God and then, one day, *"he was not."* His relationship with God was so intimate that God simply took him up to Heaven. We need to get to know God just for who He is and not only for His benefits to us. When our hearts are right toward God, when we love, honor, and reverence Him, we will receive His benefits, too.

He is a big God—big enough to take care of our little problems. The great English preacher from the early part of the 20th century, Smith Wigglesworth, said that we must look at earth's problems from Heaven's viewpoint.

God is alive and well today, and He sits upon His throne in Heaven!

Part II

Marietta Davis

Chapter Seven

A VISION OF HEAVEN

MARIETTA DAVIS, A 25-YEAR-OLD AMERICAN woman, living in Berlin, New York, fell into a trance for nine days during the summer of 1848. Neither her doctors nor her family could awaken her. Although she was a member of the Baptist Church in Berlin, before she entered this trance-like state, she had felt troubled and doubtful about where she would spend eternity; however, when she emerged from the trance, she was filled with joy and praise to God over what she had seen. She faithfully related her experience to her pastor, J.L. Scott. Her vision particularly described the presence of babies and children in Heaven and the provision that God has made for them there.

Marietta declared that during those nine days, she visited the "eternal realm." She knew that she did not have much time left on earth, and she would soon be returning to Heaven to live in the mansion Jesus had prepared for her. Seven months later, at a time she had predicted, she died, singing a hymn with her family. The following narrative reveals what she experienced, as she, too, saw Heaven.[7]

One to Show the Way

As she entered this trance, Marietta's ability to see the natural world faded away, and she seemed to be floating over a great expanse. She felt somewhat afraid and wondered to herself if there was anyone to guide her through this vast, unknown region.

Suddenly, far away and slightly above her, she saw a bright light, similar to a star. Marietta felt herself drawn toward this light whose brightness seemed to give her new life and strength. Ascending toward it in space, she began to make out an outline of what appeared to be a human-like figure. She realized it was an angel, perfect and extraordinarily beautiful, which was moving close to her.

This angel had a crown of jewels, and it radiated with the light of God's love. The angel's left hand held a cross, and its right hand grasped a scepter of light. The angel touched this wand to Marietta's lips, and it awoke a desire within Marietta to know this being.

The angel spoke to Marietta, identifying itself as the angel of peace, sent to guide her and show her those from earth who had come to live in Heaven. First, however, this messenger revealed to Marietta her own body back on earth, surrounded by worried friends and family, trying to revive her. The angel explained that on earth, death approaches and brings fear and unrest to mankind. Marietta then replied that these very thoughts had troubled her to no end and inquired if there really was a place of rest for those who had departed.

Close to Death

The angel began to explain that many who had died lived in joy and light, clothed in white garments, in a place where there was no sorrow or suffering. Others, however, did not experience this.

The angel opened Marietta's vision to a multitude of people, some rich, some poor, others in prison, yet others left alone, who were all at the point of death. As each died, various types of spirits gathered around them and escorted them either to places of darkness or to the place of brightness toward which the angel was beckoning Marietta.

Marietta moved toward a cloud of light and began to see beings of pure light moving as fast as human thought. The angel told her that these were the ministering angels, which were engaged in errands of mercy, protecting and guarding those on earth.

One of these ministering angels came near Marietta, holding an "infant" spirit, which appeared to feel peace and security in the hands of its protector. Asking from where the child had come, she was told that the ministering angel had just received it from a brokenhearted mother upon the child's death and that he was being taken to the area for infants.

From there, Marietta and the angelic spirit passed through an arch of fruit-bearing trees, filled with singing birds. Thinking she was on a physical planet, Marietta asked its name and was told that she was actually in the outer part of Heaven, and a lower part at that! The angel explained that the groves of trees moved with worship of God and that the songs of the birds revealed the greatness of God's love.

According to the angel, when those who are Christ's enter paradise, they are brought to this outer area first by their own guardian angels and taught about Heaven's ways—the praises and pure love they will offer to their Savior. Friends who have already begun to understand and experience Heaven's realities welcome these "newcomers."

Then the angel revealed the purpose of Marietta's visit; she was here for a short time to learn what happens to God's children when they depart from earth. Plucking a rose that hung overhead, the angel handed it to Marietta. Upon inhaling its fragrance, Marietta's perception was opened still further, and she saw the many joyful beings who passed through this outer area. Although she wanted a chance to speak with them, the angel took her upward through beautiful forests.

Chapter Eight

THE HEAVENLY CITY

As MARIETTA LOOKED OUT INTO the distance, she saw what appeared to be a dome of light, setting on a higher plane. The angel told her that it was the gateway that led to the heavenly City—the City of Peace. She would be able to see Jesus, the Redeemer, there; and it was the home of the saints and angels who sing the songs of redemption, love, and peace.

Drawing near, Marietta heard the praises that the saints and angels spoke, which blended into a song of divine love. A group of extremely beautiful attendants surrounded the gateway to the city, and one spoke to Marietta's angel in a language she did not understand, but which sounded like music.

A gate made of jasper and surrounded by diamonds opened, and two angels approached, taking Marietta by the hand and leading her toward an inner gate. As they moved with her toward an open area filled with light, her mind became troubled at the thought of her sins, doubts, and rebellion. She was downcast, feeling unworthy to enter a place filled with such glory.

She Beholds Jesus!

The angels brought her to the feet of a Being so glorious, wearing a crown of light. He was so lovely that she could find no words to express it.

One of the angels spoke, telling her that this was her Redeemer who had died for her. Marietta bowed before Him, wishing she were worthy to praise Him. He stretched His hand out to her and raised her up, speaking in a voice that filled her with joy. Jesus called her His child and welcomed her, calling upon those spirits around her to receive her as a companion.

The angels, who had been worshiping Him, rose and humbly welcomed Marietta and then began to sing praises to Him who was the Lamb of God. The entire dome of this pavilion of light was filled with their music, which sounded to her as the "voice of many waters" mentioned in Revelation 14:2. As the angels sang their praises, they played golden harps, producing a sound that swelled as the ocean over all who were there.

Meeting with Friends

As Marietta joined in the praise and worship, one of the spirits approached her and addressed her by name, as if speaking to a friend. Marietta found herself being embraced and welcomed by a person whom she had loved as closely as a sister while on earth. With her were other close friends who wanted to greet Marietta. She sat with them in seats much like those of an amphitheater in that room.

Although she had known these people very well while she was on earth, Marietta noticed a change in their appearance. The only way she could describe it was as if they were "all mind," filled with glory, light, joy, and love. They *spoke* with each other, but did not use human language or even sound. Their thoughts seemed to move from spirit to spirit. Marietta began to realize that in Heaven nothing is "hidden," as she was able to understand from them the nature of their lives here.

The spirits of these friends began to sing a song of praise to God, and Marietta's angel urged her to join in. She, however, was so caught up in the contemplation of this place of rest for which she had hoped, that she could not. Her angel then touched her lips again with the wand of light and invited her to speak with those present.

These spirits embraced her, and Marietta was amazed at the glory upon their faces and the lack of the signs of age and infirmity she had seen in life. She realized that the best efforts of people of God to explain and describe Heaven fell far short of its reality!

A Pilgrim Spirit

Someone she had known on earth as old and gray-headed approached Marietta, but was now transformed into a strong, vigorous youth. This pilgrim described the power of God's grace that had transformed him from one who struggled with sin and lived in a frail, mortal body to one who was redeemed from sin and death. He loudly proclaimed the worthiness of God and of Jesus when a group of tiny children joined him, holding hands and raising their voices with him in praise.

The Cross

As this song drew to an end, Marietta saw the dome above her open and a bright light descended, filled with beings even more glorious than those she had seen. Although she wanted to run from this light, her angel spoke to her, revealing that this was the glory of the cross that was descending upon her.

A cross appeared with the words "Patriarchs, Prophets, and Apostles" written upon it. Above the cross appeared the words "Jesus of Nazareth, King of the Jews." At the foot of the cross bowed an adoring spirit dressed in white garments. The angel then told Marietta that Jesus had allowed her to be admitted there even though she would soon have to return to earth, bearing a message of God's love. The angel further revealed that Marietta would have a message for a young man who was still on earth and wandering in darkness.

The angel began to tell Marietta that though she felt sorrow at leaving Heaven, she would carry great riches of truth back to earth. Marietta would be able to tell others that the cross is honored in Heaven, that all humans do indeed have guardian angels who watch constantly for them, and that as Jesus' return approached, all mankind would begin to be aware of the reality of Heaven.

After leading a hymn of praise that was beyond human comprehension, the spirit reminded Marietta that only through Christ the Redeemer could any person have the hope of Heaven. Marietta once again remembered her sins and doubts, and her spirit was saddened. She cried out that she would give everything to be able to live forever in this place of eternal peace and love.

The spirit encouraged her to be faithful to the truth she had been shown and that she, too, would know the joy of Heaven forever.

Chapter Nine

CHILDREN IN HEAVEN

THE ANGEL HELD OUT HER hands, and two children drew close to her. She introduced them to Marietta, saying that they both had died while very young and due to their innocence had been brought to the infant area of Heaven. The older of the two children expressed his gladness that Marietta was with them because when she returned to earth, Marietta would be able to comfort their parents with the great joy the children now experienced. These children knew that unlike Heaven, earth was filled with sorrow and death.

Suddenly, another angel passed above them, and Marietta asked who it was. The angel told her that it was another angel who belonged to the "infant Heaven," a guardian of these little ones who met them as soon as they left the earthly world and entered the spiritual one. Marietta then saw a very small, faint light. When the angel breathed upon this light, it was revealed to be an infant at rest. And as suddenly as it had appeared, the angel, and infant with her, disappeared.

From Earth's Viewpoint

Marietta then saw a far different scene. Below her, she beheld a woman weeping over the body of her lifeless child, whose cheek she kissed. A man entered the room, attempting to comfort this mother with the Scriptures that tell of God's care for children.

The scene moved to the funeral for the dead child, where the mother's face was filled with despair. The same man stood before the child's casket, reading from Psalms and exhorting those present to believe from the Bible that the child lived in Heaven, taken there by an angel.

This picture faded, and one of the two children with Marietta told her that the child in the vision was himself. The woman was his own mother, and the man was a minister. The angel they had seen was the very one who had escorted him to a special nursery in Heaven prepared for infants. Did Marietta want to visit that place?

Beauty and Harmony

Marietta, the angel, and the two children began to ascend to a beautiful city surrounded by flowers and filled with stately buildings, shady trees, and colorful, melodious birds. The farther they went, the more beautiful and harmonious the buildings and the whole atmosphere became. The numerous avenues led to a central area where there was a building that appeared to be constructed of delicately carved marble. It supported a vast dome.

This was the home of all the infants in Heaven. Along the avenues, there had been other buildings. These were the "nurseries" where infants were first brought and instructed in the truths of Heaven.

This angelic servant proceeded to explain that when an infant died on earth, the guardian angel escorted him to Heaven and grouped him with others of similar artistic, scientific, and social abilities, where that child could best develop. There were seven guardian angels over each building who directed the infants' instruction, and the buildings themselves were grouped into "families" of seven. This method of organization allowed for an orderly instruction of the little children, who were brought together to sing the praises of their Savior.

Marietta was then allowed to see into the nurseries and felt that she had indeed seen Heaven! In the nurseries, these babies were lovingly tended and instructed by angels, who also played the most beautiful music imaginable for the tiny ones with whom they had been entrusted. Marietta's angel expressed her fervent wish that bereaved parents on earth could know the love and care that awaited their children in Heaven!

Chapter Ten

Jesus and the Little Ones

As Marietta's angel was speaking, the guardian angels, with their infants, rose and joined the choir surrounding the angel who held the cross. A great light descended from above and in the midst of the angels was Jesus.

The groups of angels and infants approached Him, and He said, "Let the little children come to Me, and do not forbid them" (see Matt. 19:14). He moved His hand over them, and goodness, like drops of water, rained down upon them. These infants seemed to drink as if from a fountain of living water. The angels who attended Him began to sing a hymn of redemption, and music arose from every temple in the city. As the music rose, Jesus re-ascended to His place.

Next, Marietta and her angel approached the area where she would see the infants who were just arriving from earth.

Chapter Eleven

SUFFERING ON THE CROSS

As Marietta looked at the face of the angel who was leading her, she thought the angel looked as if she would weep. Marietta wondered to herself if sorrow could indeed enter Heaven. The angel seemed transfixed by some scene, and she lifted Marietta's head and pointed to what held her attention.

To Marietta's great shock, she beheld a vision of the cross upon which Jesus had hung, suffering and dying! There were guardian angels and their infant spirits gathered in a circle, worshiping the Lord in reverent silence. Each infant was brought near the cross, where a stream of light touched them. A heavenly choir began to sing, and the cross and its sacrifice disappeared from view.

Marietta's angel began to explain to her that the cross was always in the sight of those who had been redeemed, and that it was constantly impressed upon the infants there so that they would fully understand and appreciate the sacrifice of their Redeemer.

Chapter Twelve

VISIONS OF HEAVEN, VISIONS OF HELL

SUDDENLY MARIETTA HEARD A VOICE saying, "Come up here." Looking up, she saw a circular pathway winding upward. She and the angel passed along this spiral on a cloud of light into a rainbow-colored tower. As they emerged from this path, they stood on a high plain, where Marietta could see the City of God on every side. Below her was the center temple of instruction. It was built of precious materials in a style of architecture beyond human description.

The temple rose from a circular lawn that was the most intense green. This lawn was filled with groups of large trees that bore fragrant flowers. Under the shade of the trees were beds of every type of flower, shrub, and vine. She could see fountains of living water. The water in some of the fountains was caught in basins made of diamonds, burnished silver, or white pearl.

An open trellis, on whose eastern side a door-less gateway appeared, surrounded the lawn. From the center of the gateway a stream of living water flowed from the fountains inside. The river of living waters divided the city into 12 sections. The river was bordered on either side by a wide avenue, intersected by 12 other streets.

The city was divided into 144 "wards" that were arranged in increasing degrees of beauty. From the outer boundary to the center, there was an ascending pathway of increasing loveliness, marked by more beautiful and different trees, flowers, fountains, statues, and buildings. The whole city appeared to be one garden of flowers, one grove, one gallery of sculpture, one sea of fountains, all set in a beautiful landscape. The sky above was filled with a divine light that colored every object.

Marietta could now see the movement of those who inhabited the city, and it was marked by perfect peace. She saw neither rivalry nor selfishness among the infants in the place. Instead, each little child was filled with a holy love and a desire to learn. As she watched, each child unfolded like a flower from beauty to greater beauty.

From seeing the city of infant Heaven in its entire splendor, Marietta's vision then widened to where she could see all the angels gathered around the various buildings. Her angel explained that these infants would go on to schools of higher instruction, and Marietta would be allowed to see them. First, however, she was to have a vision of a far different sort.

Separated from God

Marietta found herself in the abyss, where those spirits who have rejected Christ dwell. How different it was from Heaven. There, she saw a suffering multitude indulging their passions—the same passions they had cultivated while still in their bodies. One she had known on earth approached her to explain that the beings there were filled with sorrow and all the effects of evil. She learned that sin brings death and that there is no happiness to be found in disobedience to God, but only in faith in Jesus as Savior. It was with great relief that she again heard a voice calling her to "Come up here!"

As she reflected upon what she had seen, another being clothed in garments as bright as the sun addressed her. This angelic spirit told her to rest and to dismiss her anxious thoughts over what she had just seen. She was assured that God had indeed prepared a mansion in Heaven for those who were His. She was then warned that every person whose heart is not established in truth and whose nature is not controlled by the love of God is subject to the attraction of evil.

This angel further admonished Marietta that all who wish to gain Heaven and avoid hell must turn from wicked desires and cling to God and to His truth.

Again beholding the beauty and glory of the infant nursery, Marietta was allowed to hear the heavenly music of the infant choirs, which joined to create an atmosphere of God's love and perfect order.

The Life of Jesus

Marietta began to receive instruction by a series of visions in which she was allowed to see the earthly ministry of Jesus. She saw the babe born to Mary in the holy city of Bethlehem; she watched His betrayal by Judas; she stood near as He prayed in the Garden and as the Romans took him prisoner. She saw the mockery of His trial and His humiliation, and finally, she beheld His crucifixion. But Marietta also beheld His resurrection and

His defeat of death. She watched as He ascended into Heaven and heard the praises of His mother Mary and of the disciples. This series of visions taught her more of His love and the eternal truth of His death, resurrection, and ascension into Heaven.

Return to Earth

As these visions faded, the angel and the two children approached Marietta. They consoled her because she had to leave Heaven for a while and return to earth, but they rejoiced with her that she would return at the appointed time. Moreover, they rejoiced that she had been allowed to see the plan for man's redemption and had been received by the Savior. The spirit and the two children embraced Marietta and asked her to tell their loved ones still on earth of the joys and pleasures they knew in Heaven.

Then, Jesus Himself descended from a cloud and placed His hand upon Marietta's head. He charged her to be faithful to relate what she had seen and heard and to fulfill her mission. He promised her that at the appointed time, angels would bear her to the mansion prepared for her. He admonished her not to be sad, but to allow His grace to sustain her.

She bowed and worshiped her Savior, who handed her an olive branch and told her to take it to earth as she had been instructed.

Marietta was carried away in the arms of the angels to the gateway of Heaven. Accompanied by the angel that had guided her, she descended to earth, entered the room where her body lay, and awoke!

Marietta faithfully told what had been revealed to her in Heaven. She went into great detail about her vision with her pastor, J.L. Scott, who was impressed with the Christlikeness and holiness of her story. Her brief remainder of life was marked by her strong hope of Heaven and her joy that she would spend eternity there.

However, as she had been told during her vision, she was not to remain on earth for much longer. She had been promised that she would soon return to Heaven for good. In March 1849, just seven months after her vision, Marietta Davis died, leaving behind a remarkable testimony to Heaven's reality.

Part III

REBECCA SPRINGER

Chapter Thirteen

A Home in Heaven

Rebecca Springer, a young wife, lay close to death in Kentville, Canada, for nearly three weeks, surrounded by untrained strangers. They did their best to help her, but she received no nourishment and little water. At times, she would lose consciousness. Although she longed for her loved ones, she would not call upon them to come to her, and neglect their responsibilities. Instead, she called upon Christ to sustain her with His presence, and amidst her suffering, she experienced His peace.

One dark morning, it seemed to Rebecca that she stood on the floor by her bed, in front of the large stained-glass window that opened onto a veranda overlooking the street. Sensing someone near her, she looked up to see her husband's favorite brother, Frank, who had died many years before. After she expressed her joy at seeing him, her brother-in-law asked her if she was ready to go, and drew her toward the window. Rebecca believed that she was about to depart this life forever and begged Frank to let her stay. He replied that he would do so a bit later, once she had rested, for she was worn from her sickness. Gazing down at her own form on the bed, she agreed to go with him.

Rebecca Springer's vision of Heaven confirms that those we have loved who have died in the Lord will know us, and we will know them and rejoice with them in an eternity of worship and praise to the Savior of the world.[8]

Beholding Heaven

As Frank and Rebecca moved up the street, she turned and looked back several times, hesitating to leave earth. Frank picked Rebecca up as if she were a child, and she felt tremendous relief at having someone to care for her after her ordeal.

The next thing she knew, Rebecca was sitting in a sheltered area of flowering shrubs upon soft, green grass blossoming with fragrant flowers, some of which she recognized from earth and others which were new to her. She observed how perfect each plant was with smooth, glossy leaves. Stretching into the distance was a field of perfect grass, flowers, and trees bearing blossoms and fruits. It reminded her of the tree of life in Revelation 22:2 that bore 12 kinds of fruit.

Under the trees, she saw groups of happy little children playing, catching brightly colored birds that seemed to play along with them. Older people walked through the grounds bearing a tangible air of peace and happiness. Everyone she saw was wearing pure white clothing. Looking farther, she saw beautiful homes of unusual design, sparkling fountains, and a river clear as crystal. The walkways appeared to be made of pearl. Everything spoke to her of purity for there was no decay. The air was fresh and invigorating, and instead of sunlight, there was a golden glow similar to a summer sunset.

The River

Rebecca and Frank reached the river of life. It was lined with beautiful stones, but was not cold; rather, it felt very much like the surrounding air. At that moment, Rebecca looked down and was delighted to see that she, too, was clothed in the white raiment of Heaven.

She didn't want to venture farther into the water, exclaiming that it would cover her head and she might drown. Frank gently reminded her that there was no death in Heaven. Plunging into the river, Rebecca found she could breathe—and talk and see, just as if she were above the water. Frank encouraged her to run her hands over her face and through her hair. She did, and it was a delightful feeling, although she regretted the tangles in her long hair she was sure to have once they left the water. Besides, what would they do for towels?

Emerging from the river, she realized that as soon as the air touched her, her skin, hair, and clothing were as dry as before they entered the water. In fact, her robe seemed even more beautiful than when she had entered the river. She felt as if she could fly and asked Frank what the water had done for her.

Frank replied that the river of life had washed away the last influences of life on earth and had made her ready for her new life in Heaven.

The Heavenly Mansion

As Rebecca and Frank walked on, they approached beautiful houses made of fine marble, surrounded by vast verandas. She had never seen this type of architecture before, and the flowers and vines were far more beautiful that anything of which she might have dreamed. She saw joyful faces looking out at her and heard happy voices from the homes.

Upon being asked where they were going, Frank explained that he and Rebecca were going home. He led her to a beautiful house of light gray marble sheltered by graceful green trees. To her surprise, she heard a well-loved voice exclaim her joy in being the first to welcome Rebecca. It was a dear friend, Mrs. Wickham, who embraced Rebecca warmly. Frank and Rebecca invited her in, but she insisted on waiting until later, reminding them that they had all eternity!

Frank led Rebecca up the stairs to the veranda and into the house between large marble columns. The reception hall had an inlaid floor, a window with mullioned glass, and a wide, low stairway. Before Rebecca could speak, Frank took her hands and welcomed her to her heavenly home. It was to be for Rebecca and Frank's brother, once he came. He led her into a large room made of polished, pale gray marble. The walls and floors, however, were covered with beautiful roses of every type and color. Attempting to gather some up so she would not crush them, Rebecca found them to be embedded in the marble! Frank explained to her that a group of boys and girls had come to the house one day asking if it really were for the Springers. Upon being told that it was, they replied that they had loved the couple and wanted to help make the house even more beautiful. The girls, who carried bouquets of roses, began to toss them over the floors and against the walls, where they remained attached, giving the appearance of fresh flowers. The boys produced tool cases and through some celestial art, embedded each flower in the marble.

Rebecca asked Frank who these young people were, and he named them for her. She realized that her love for these children on earth had brought her additional happiness in Heaven.

Constructed for Eternity

Frank showed Rebecca through the library filled with rare and costly books. The room contained stained-glass windows and a writing desk. Upon the desk sat a golden bowl filled with carnations—the favorite flowers of Rebecca's husband. She realized that in Heaven, the tastes of those things we loved on earth are never forgotten. Inquiring as to why there should be books in Heaven, Rebecca was told that the pure and good desires of the soul remained, and that some of these books had been written on earth in such a way as to lift the human mind to a higher plane. Others had been written in Heaven to express the great truths found there. Heaven was to be a place of increased knowledge and understanding.

Life in Heaven

As Frank took Rebecca through the rest of the house, she noticed that each room was distinct, yet perfect and beautiful. A room had been set aside for her personal rest and study on the second floor, which was finished with inlaid woods rather than the light gray marble. This special room of Rebecca's was oblong, with large windows, and fitted with an ivory desk. Ivory bookshelves stood across from the desk, filled with volumes by some of her favorite authors. The furniture was constructed of ivory with silver gray upholstery. She found the room to be indescribably beautiful.

Frank and Rebecca then passed through an open window onto a marble terrace with a staircase that wound down to the lawn. Tree branches filled with ripe fruit hung close to the terrace. Some of the fruits seemed to resemble those on earth, only with a far superior consistency and flavor. Although she bit into a fruit similar to a pear, and its juice ran off her hands and down her dress, there were no stains left on her clothing and her hands were as clean as if she had washed them. Frank explained that no impurity could remain in Heaven's environment. Rebecca realized that this was the explanation for why no fruit lay under the trees.

Descending with her to the room filled with the inlaid roses, Frank asked Rebecca who she wanted to see most of all of those she knew in Heaven. She quickly answered that she wished to see her parents. Then, as she turned around, she saw her mother, father, and youngest sister coming toward her. The tender reunion filled them all with joy. Frank then departed to take care of other work and left her in the care of her parents, reminding them that she needed to rest, for it was not only one of the joys, but one of the duties of those who had entered Heaven.

Chapter Fourteen

LOVED ONES IN HEAVEN

As Rebecca became comfortable with Heaven, she found wonderful surprises waiting everywhere. She frequently would come upon old friends—many of whom had departed earth years before, and she was also overjoyed to meet many whom she had never expected to meet in Heaven. Several of these were people whom her words and acts had helped steer from a life of sin into eternal life.

Further Reunions

On her way to the river of life, Rebecca saw a young girl run toward her with her arms outstretched. It was her niece, Mae, who radiated joy and beauty. Mae explained that it was not only the divine life in Heaven that had transformed her; it was the frequent nearness to the Savior. Mae expressed her gratitude to Jesus and her great love for Him. She had come to love Him above all things and counted being near to Him as more important than anything else.

Upon Rebecca's asking her to accompany her to the river, Mae inquired if she had ever been to the lake or the sea. Rebecca joined her on the path to the lake. As they walked along, Mae asked when her Uncle Will, Rebecca's husband, would be joining them. Although she was not discontent, she longed to see the rest of her family and assured Rebecca that in Heaven, the wait for loved ones never seemed long.

The Glory of Heaven

Arriving at the lake, Mae pointed to it and asked Rebecca if it wasn't "divinely beautiful." Rebecca had to cover her eyes because of the glory of that place, as she was not yet strong enough spiritually to look at it. As Mae encouraged her to behold it, she saw a lake as smooth as glass filled with flowers and fruit-bearing trees, and in the distance, Rebecca could see what appeared to be a city.

There were many people resting on the banks of the river and several boats were on the water, filled with happy people. Little children and adults floated in the water, while singing angels drifted overhead, their voices lifted in praise. Mae seized Rebecca's hand to hasten her to join them.

As they stood upon the bank, tears of rapture fell down Rebecca's face. Mae led her down to the water into its depths. After sinking to what felt like hundreds of feet below the surface, both women lay prostrate and began to rise until a current below the surface pulled them along. Rebecca watched a changing panorama of beautiful colored lights.

Music of Heaven

Rebecca began to hear the distant sound of music. Presently the words became clear. It was a song of adoration to Jesus sung by the angel choir. She also heard the sweet tones of a bell. Mae explained to her that not only did the waters of the lake catch and reflect light, but it also did the same with music from a great distance. The bell summoned them to heavenly duties.

As they listened to the notes of the bell, a great peace came over Rebecca and she slept, to later awaken to a sense of renewed strength. The lake had filled her with the divine life itself. As she emerged from the water, Rebecca realized that even though children and animals played around the waters of the lake, there was no anxiety or fear of an accident. Instead, there was a sense of safety and security.

As Mae began to relate her experiences in Heaven, Rebecca was seized with a longing to see Jesus. She asked Mae when she would see her Savior. The girl replied that it would not be long, for He would not delay.

Chapter Fifteen

JESUS!

AFTER HER RETURN FROM THE lake, Frank asked Rebecca if she cared to visit her friend Mrs. Wickham. They were soon on their way to her beautiful home, where Rebecca was shown through the house, marveling at each lovely room and its furnishings. They discussed Mrs. Wickham's daughter, who frequently performed upon the instruments found in one of the rooms. After a while, the conversation turned to those still on earth whom Mrs. Wickham had known.

Rebecca's hostess rose, but asked her to stay, remarking that she would return quickly. Rebecca noticed a stranger at the front entrance who seemed familiar. He had a sweet and beautiful face, and she thought it must be John the beloved disciple.

As he entered, he said, "Peace be unto this house." Although Rebecca began to call for Mrs. Wickham, the guest asked her to sit and talk with him for a while. They began to discuss her recent arrival, and Rebecca remarked how much she wanted to see Him whom she loved. Suddenly, the guest looked into her eyes with such love that she realized who He was. It was Jesus!

She embraced Him, and He wiped away the tears that had formed in her eyes. He comforted the fears that she had and began to explain the mysteries of Heaven to her. Rebecca literally drank in His words as if she could not get enough. Finally, He rose to depart, telling her that they would meet often and laying His hands in blessing upon her head.

Watching Jesus as He passed beneath the trees outside, Rebecca saw two young girls approach Him. She knew who they were—Mary Bates and Mae Camden. Flying to meet Him with great joy, they took His hands and accompanied Him on His way. Rebecca realized that they were like younger children with a dearly loved elder brother.

Mrs. Wickham appeared, and she knew that Rebecca's heart was very full from her encounter with Jesus. Gently leading her to the door, she allowed Rebecca to go without speaking.

Arriving at home, Rebecca found Frank sitting on the veranda. One look at her face told him that she had been with Jesus. Rebecca hurried to the solitude of her room where she relived each moment she had spent in His presence. She began to thank God for this privilege and then joined Frank in praise to her Creator.

Chapter Sixteen

MARY BATES

As Rebecca went in search of some of her former friends, she heard a young voice calling out to her. It was a family friend, Mary Bates. Mary was thrilled to see Rebecca and told her that Jesus had revealed that she was in Heaven. Jesus had told Mary and Mae that they should spend time with Rebecca quite often.

Mary wanted to hear about her own mother still on earth. She wished her mother could know her daughter's joy in Heaven; what a burden would be lifted from her. Rebecca and Mary walked together, talking about those they had known on earth and answering one another's questions. They came upon a group of four people—three women and a man. They recognized that the man was Jesus. One of the women seemed to have just arrived, and Jesus took her hand as He talked to her. The three women listened closely to His words. Just then, Jesus turned and looked at Rebecca and Mary. His tender, encouraging look lifted and blessed them both. Later, when they could speak of it, Mary said that if Jesus was too busy with someone else to speak, He simply looked at you, and that was enough!

The Compassion of Jesus

Mary explained to Rebecca that Jesus' face was the first she saw after she left her body. At first, she felt shy and anxious around Him, but He encouraged her to trust Him, and her fear left. She found Him to be full of the same tender care as her own brothers.

Returning to her home and entering her room, the two friends sat in peace as Mary told Rebecca how glad she was that the other had come to Heaven.

Rebecca also noticed another feature of Heaven—just as the Scriptures say, there is no darkness or night in Heaven. The radiant glory of God filled every part of Heaven during what might be called day. Later, there would be no darkness or shadows, just a softening of that glory.

Chapter Seventeen

A Speech in Heaven

Not too long after Rebecca's encounter with Mary Bates, Frank told her that they were to go to the great auditorium to hear Martin Luther speak about the Reformation, followed by a talk from John Wesley! He added that there might even be other speakers.

Rebecca had already visited this auditorium; it stood on a hill, constructed of an immense dome supported by columns of amethyst and jasper, with a platform of inlaid marble in the center.

Seats of polished cedar wood ascended on three sides to form the auditorium; behind the platform were purple drapes. Near the center of the platform stood an altar made of pearl. The dome overhead appeared dark so that only the gold carvings at its base were visible.

Entering the building, Rebecca and Frank found the congregation eagerly waiting as an invisible choir provided soft music. Soon, Martin Luther ascended the steps. She noticed that his intellect and spiritual strength amplified his physical presence;

even in Heaven, he appeared to be a capable leader. He spoke with power and eloquence, and when he finished, John Wesley took his place, speaking on the theme of "God's Love," demonstrating what it had done for mankind and how praise and thanks even into eternity could never repay that love.

After Wesley finished, a silence fell upon those present, until the purple curtains behind the platform parted. Jesus stepped out upon the platform, and all those present burst forth in a hymn of praise to Him. Above the voices of the redeemed, the angel choir could be heard, and the glory of God filled the auditorium. Then, the hymn came to an end and all sank to their knees in worship. As their praises died away, they quietly made their way back to their places. Mary Bates remained in an attitude of adoration, and Jesus looked upon her with love. Mary then slipped back into her place, and Rebecca wondered how men could have been so blind on earth as to have *crucified the Lord of glory*" (see 1 Cor. 2:8).

The Savior's Voice

Jesus began to speak, and His voice was far sweeter than the sound of the angel choir. Rebecca could find no earthly words to express what He said. He spoke about the link between life on earth and life in Heaven and then revealed the wonderful duties that lay before the redeemed. After He spoke, those present sat with bowed heads in silence. Rebecca found her heart repeating, "Amen and amen" to the Savior's words.

Chapter Eighteen

SISTER AND FRIEND

As REBECCA BEGAN TO CROSS the lawn between her house and her father's, she heard her name called out. Turning, she saw a tall, noble-looking man with white hair and deep blue eyes approaching her. It was Oliver, the husband of her eldest sister.

Oliver had not known that Rebecca had come until just moments before. He greeted her warmly and expressed his gratitude that she had been able to come before his wife (her sister, Lu) had come to Heaven. Rebecca asked if Lu were to come soon, but Oliver did not know. Still, he felt that her arrival could not be too far away. Rebecca accompanied her brother-in-law to his home, itself another example of the perfection of Heaven. She returned often to visit him there and to plan for Lu's coming.

She met a group of children and recognized them as Lu's grandchildren. They greeted her joyfully, shouting that their grandmother was coming, and they were taking flowers to scatter to welcome her.

Rebecca asked how they knew Lu was coming, and they replied that their grandfather, Oliver, had sent word to them and that he was to bring her. Rebecca hurried to her father's house and found the rest of her family waiting for her; they had already heard the news. Frank joined them on their way to welcome this beloved sister to her home.

Tender Reunion

Entering the house, Rebecca saw her sister standing with her husband and grandchildren. But she was astonished to see her. Could this radiant woman be the same person who had appeared so pale and marked by suffering? It was indeed her sister, but looking as she had 30 years earlier, full of health.

Rebecca's heart was filled with the certainty of Christ's victory over death as she beheld her sister. After all the others had greeted Lu, Rebecca embraced her and they rejoiced together. Oliver was filled with joy at the moment for which he had waited and longed. Lu wept with joy at her beautiful room, declaring it a much greater gain for the loss of earth!

He explained to Rebecca that he had taken his wife to the river first, and as she sat in the water, the years rolled away from her. Rebecca commented that she saw new life in Oliver. He asked her if she was aware of the change that had come to her since she had entered Heaven. Rebecca rejoiced at this further evidence of God's love and goodness.

A Special Friend

After leaving her parents, Rebecca walked toward the lake, longing for a rest in the waters after the excitement of her sister's arrival. There were only a few people on the shore when she arrived, and the boats speeding across the waters seemed filled with messengers who had a duty to perform. Walking slowly into the waters, Rebecca found herself floating in the current. The rays that were refracted by the water blended into beautiful colors, more glorious to her eyes than a rainbow.

She heard the bell in the city ringing out an anthem, which seemed to say, "Holy, holy, holy," and the waters of the lake took up the song and responded to it. Rebecca lay and listened to this great chorus and joined with them in praise.

The Far Shore

Rebecca found that she had floated away from the point where she had entered the lake and was drifting toward part of the shore that she had not visited. She climbed the banks to find herself in the middle of a small village. Although it reminded her of Switzerland, it was far more beautiful.

She came upon a particularly attractive house, where a woman sat beneath the trees nearby, weaving a white, delicate fabric. This woman somehow appeared familiar, and as she looked up, Rebecca recognized her and called her name, Maggie. They greeted one another warmly, and Rebecca realized why she had come that way; it was to find her friend. They talked comfortably with more ease than they ever had on earth. Rebecca asked her friend what she was weaving. Maggie replied that she was weaving draperies for her daughter Nellie's room and promised to show Rebecca how to do it. Rebecca rejoiced, not only to have found her friend, but also to be able to help Maggie decorate Nellie's windows and thus give her pleasure.

Chapter Nineteen

THE CITY OF GOD

ON ONE OF HER WALKS, Rebecca came upon a group of children at the lakeshore, clustered around Jesus. He held one tiny girl in His arms, and she rested her head against Him, her hands filled with the water lilies that floated upon the lake. Others sat at His feet or leaned against Him. One boy stood next to Jesus with his arm around His shoulder as Jesus encircled him with His right arm.

Jesus was telling them a story, and every one of them was transfixed as they listened to Him. Rebecca heard bits of the story, enough to know that Jesus was telling them about His care and protection of children. One child spoke up that if he had ever been in danger from wild animals on earth, he would have prayed to Jesus to shut the mouths of the beasts just as He did for Daniel in the lions' den. Rebecca thought how comforted that child's parents could be if they could see the tender, loving look Jesus gave the boy as he made his reply. Suddenly she heard a happy shout from the children as His story reached a satisfying ending.

The City by the Lake

As Rebecca started for home, she met Frank who asked her if she would like to visit the city by the lake. Rebecca replied that she had long wanted to go there but had waited until Frank thought she was ready. He replied that she had learned Heaven's ways so quickly that he could now take her anywhere with him. He told her that her desire to learn of Heaven out of love for God had won her the praise of Jesus Himself. Frank told her that he felt that Jesus would soon entrust her with a mission in Heaven.

Rebecca was so overjoyed to hear this that she could barely speak. She and Frank walked silently back to the edge of the lake and entered a boat, which took them to the farthest shore. The boat took them up to a marble terrace that was the entrance to the city. They passed up a hill and found themselves on a broad street that led to the center of the city. The streets were wide and paved with marble and precious stones. Although there was a multitude of people going about their business, there was no debris or even any dust.

Rebecca observed buildings very much like business offices and colleges, schools, book and music stores, publishing houses, factories, art galleries, libraries, lecture halls, and auditoriums. However, she saw no churches, and this puzzled her until she remembered that in Heaven, all were united in the worship of the Father and the Son; there were no separate denominations there. She wished that this same atmosphere of united worship to Him could dominate earth. How much jealousy and rivalry would be eliminated!

She saw no homes in the middle of the city, but only in the suburbs. Each home had a large garden, filled with trees and flowers. The whole city was covered with gardens to the point that it was more like an enormous park sprinkled with houses. Before she and Frank left, Rebecca noticed an immense open pavilion where the seraph choir had just sung. She and Frank determined to return again to hear that choir and its heavenly music.

Chapter Twenty

THE TEMPLE OF GOD

FRANK AND REBECCA CAME OUT into open country and walked through meadows and plains and then entered a great forest. Even though the trees were close together in this dense wood, the glow of the heavenly light filled it.

Emerging from the forest into a great plain, they became aware of an enormous temple with a dome, pillars, and walls made of solid pearl. A white radiance shown through the windows of this temple. Rebecca sank to her knees and began to worship Him in stillness with her whole heart. Even in Heaven, "time" turned to nothing as she knelt.

Frank gently lifted her to her feet and whispered for her to come. In silence, she followed him up a flight of pearl steps to the door of the temple. They entered the temple in silence, and there she observed the immense dome, held up by three great pillars of gold. The walls, floors, and the platform on the eastern side were made of pearl. A gold railing was set around the platform on three sides so that it could not be reached from the main part of the temple. In the middle of the platform there was an immense altar of gold, supported by seraphs made of gold with their wings outstretched. Beneath the altar, a fountain danced into a pearl basin. Rebecca knew that this fountain was the source of the river of life.

The Bright Glory of His Presence

Rebecca saw two persons kneeling with their heads bowed on the far side of the temple by the altar rail. Four angels dressed in white stood by the altar with golden trumpets lifted in their hands. Suddenly, she saw the draperies behind the platform glow with a radiance greater than the sun. The temple was filled with His glory. In the cloud that filled the dome, Frank and Rebecca saw the angels with their harps. They knelt beside the altar rail with bowed heads and hid their faces from the *"brightness of his coming"* (see 2 Thess. 2:8).

The trumpet call of the four angels sounded, and the celestial choir sang, "Holy, holy, holy." As the voices died away and the trumpets sounded their last notes, Frank and Rebecca knew that God's visible presence was being withdrawn from the temple. Still, they kept their faces bowed in silence.

Leaving the temple, Rebecca found herself trembling with emotion. She and Frank returned home by way of the river.

The Journey Home

They reached the stream and stepped into a boat by the shore, heading toward home. Passing by beautiful scenes she had not seen before, Rebecca resolved to return to visit there in the future. Both sides of the shore were filled with beautiful mansions surrounded by perfect green grounds.

Frank and Rebecca were silent during most of the trip home. However, they noticed many happy domestic scenes on either side of the river, with the sounds of glad voices and happy laughter reaching them. Rebecca remarked to Frank that she was often happily surprised to hear some of the songs of earth sung in Heaven, but never more so than today; the hymn, "Holy, Holy, Holy" was one of her favorites.

Frank replied that on every possible occasion, the pure enjoyments of the earth life were reproduced in Heaven. God delighted in letting His children see that Heaven was a continuation of their former life, but without its problems and worries. As she arrived home, Rebecca's heart was filled with love, joy, and gratitude to her Father and to her Savior.

Chapter Twenty-One

More Reunions

AFTER A VISIT WITH HER friend, Mrs. Wickham, Rebecca was reunited with her Aunt Ann. She was able to tell her much about her own children and joined with her in anticipating their arrival in Heaven. Later, she was reunited with the daughter of friends, Mary Green, who immediately wanted to hear the news of all those behind on earth. Rebecca's youngest sister and Mary became immediately interested in each other, having many similar pursuits.

Reunion of Mother and Son

Rebecca maintained her studies in Heaven and continued to learn much from the journeys she took with Frank through various parts of the Kingdom of Heaven. Her time was not only filled with study and heavenly responsibilities, but with society and enjoyment. She spent much time in her father's home and on occasion, accompanied him as he instructed those who had recently entered the new life in Heaven.

Rebecca's father approached her with a problem. He was attempting to help a young man who had committed a terrible crime on earth. Infatuated by a woman, the man had killed his own mother to obtain her jewels for this creature. He had been executed for it, but had truly repented of his sins. Still, he had left the earth life with the horror of his actions still clinging to his mind and was so grateful to God for His mercy in allowing him into Heaven at all, that he was willing to stay in the very lowest sphere. Rebecca's father wanted to take him to the river of life, where the remains of the earth life might be washed away. This man had refused to see Jesus, feeling that although he was forgiven, he was unworthy to stand in His presence.

And he was not in any condition to see his mother who was there, too.

Rebecca pondered this situation and then suggested bringing his mother to him. Her father felt that this was the right decision. Rebecca lost no time in finding the mother and telling her the situation. She waited for the woman's decision. There was no hesitating; this mother longed to see her son and help him.

The two women found Rebecca's father waiting for them and accompanied him to the great house where the "students" stayed. For one just freed from earth, it seemed a perfect paradise. For those who had tasted the joys of Heaven, it lacked the individuality of each home with children playing on the lawn and the angel choir's music.

The mother approached her son who was busy studying a book Rebecca's father had given him. She cried out to him that she loved him and wanted him with her. He sobbed and knelt at her feet. She embraced him and then encouraged him to walk with her to the river. Rebecca and her father knew that the cobwebs of the earth life were soon to be washed away.

Rebecca received divine permission to work alongside her father, and this brought her even more into his company and into his wise instruction.

The Best Reunion of All

At one point, relaxing after a strenuous journey to a distant part of Heaven, Rebecca sat on the upper veranda of their home. Frank joined her, looking as weary as anyone could in Heaven, for he had been on a mission to earth. Rebecca knew that the cares and weights of earth would attempt to cling to one until the atmosphere of Heaven provided restoration.

Frank regarded Rebecca for a moment and then gently told her that he had news for her.

Instantly, a thrill like an electric shock ran through her. "He is coming!" she cried out with joy. Frank nodded and then replied that Rebecca's husband, Will, had never regained consciousness. It had happened three days before, but Frank wanted to spare Rebecca the knowledge that Will was suffering when she could do nothing to help him. Frank explained that it would not be long until Frank would need cleansing in the river of life so that his bewilderment and confusion would pass.

Rebecca decided that she would not accompany Frank, but would wait until he brought Will, already cleansed in the river of life, to her. She marveled at the grace of God that she could submit so willingly, even in a matter so close to her heart. She longed for Will's suffering to be over and for the two of them to be reunited.

Suddenly, she sensed the presence of Jesus and heard His voice. He encouraged her that the change Heaven had made in her would make the reunion with her husband better. Rebecca spoke to Him of her husband's pure Christian life and his high ideals. Jesus discussed with her the mysteries of the soul life and then told her that when she was ready to receive Will and Frank, they would arrive.

Song of Joy

As Rebecca rose to her feet following His departure, she heard the angels' triumphant song. She lifted her voice, joining with them and descended the stairway. She walked into the river of life and felt great peace. Filled with delight, she gathered a bouquet of white roses and fastened some on her garment and then refilled the golden bowl in the library with more red carnations. She fixed her hair in a style he liked and placed a white rosebud in it.

Soon, she heard voices! Rebecca flew to the door to embrace her husband. Frank thoughtfully left them alone for their reunion. She led him throughout the house, and he exclaimed over its beauty. Rebecca, Will, and Frank later sat together on the veranda and ate of the luscious fruit.

Then Rebecca told her husband and his brother that they must go to their parents. Together, they started for Father and Mother Springer's. She knew the great joy they would have at their son being reunited with them. After the visit, they met their Aunt Cynthia, who had been blind on earth, but now saw, thanks to the Master's touch. They left singing praises with great joy to God for His goodness.

Chapter Twenty-Two

THE GLASSY SEA

REBECCA WANTED TO GO TO the sea. She asked Frank about it, and he felt that it was time for her and Will to go there, although he himself would not accompany them. He instructed her how to reach it, and Rebecca and her husband set out with great joy. They emerged from the forest to stand motionless at the glorious scene before them.

A Glorious Sight

The sea was surrounded by a radiant, golden beach, and the water spread out with a brightness that exceeded description. The brightness was like the white glory that had shone through the windows of the temple, except that the blue tint of the waters was visible. The sea had no limit in its bounds or in its depths.

In every direction that they looked, they saw boats representing all nations with a beauty surpassing anything on earth. The boats were filled with people who looked eagerly toward the shore.

A vast multitude stood upon the shore, wearing the white robes of the redeemed, many of them with golden harps and musical instruments. As the boats touched shore, the passengers were welcomed with joyful voices and loving embraces. The instruments would sound and the whole company would break into a song of triumph over the grave.

A being filled with light near Rebecca told her that those on shore were the ones who expected the arrival of friends and relatives from the other life, along with those who came to share their joy.

Rebecca and Will watched the joyful reunions of friend and friend, husband and wife, mother and child. Rebecca looked out at a particularly beautiful boat and saw a man standing with his arm around a woman who stood at his side. They scanned the shore for familiar faces. Suddenly, a thrill of joy shot through Rebecca as she realized the couple was her son and his wife. They had come together! Rebecca and Will and the daughter's parents ecstatically greeted their loved ones and joined together in a hymn of praise to the One who had victory over death and the grave.

The Vision Ends

The time came when Rebecca began to feel uneasy and wondered if the care and unrest of earth had somehow entered Heaven. As she lay upon her couch, she began to hear voices, which spoke of one who had passed near death but now seemed to recover. Her vision had come to an end. The task before her now was to be faithful to tell what Jesus had told her to say, encouraging others with the blessed hope of Heaven.

Part IV

H.A. BAKER

Chapter Twenty-Three

THE VISION OF THE CHINESE BOYS

H.A. BAKER AND HIS WIFE, Josephine, served as missionaries from the United States to Tibet during the period of 1911-1919. Tibet had known periods of independence, followed by British involvement. In 1906, China had become the sovereign power of Tibet, which is located to China's southwest. During the period the Bakers were in Tibet as missionaries, the Chinese Manchu Dynasty was overthrown in 1912, and Tibet was once again declared independent, but in name only. The nation continued to experience periods of strain and conflict with China until 1950, when Communists overthrew China and invaded Tibet. In 1951, Tibet surrendered to the Communist government of mainland China and was incorporated into the Chinese nation.

Although the Bakers were told that the conversion of a Tibetan to Christianity was impossible, they persevered, learning the language and developing a great love for the people of Tibet. As the hearts of the Tibetan people opened to the good news of Jesus Christ, the possibility of a great work for God seemed imminent.

However, this was not to be. Josephine Baker's health failed her, and the couple was forced to return to America. During their stay at home, they both received the baptism in the Holy Spirit. Shortly after that, they received a letter from Allen Swift (who had prayed for them to be filled with the Holy Spirit), telling them that if they would return immediately to the mission field, his church would give them one thousand dollars for their travel expenses.

This time, the Lord directed them to go to China as faith missionaries with no denominational sponsorship. They settled in the southwest corner of Yunnan, the farthest southwest province in China, in Kotchiu, a town of about five thousand. Although they were told it was the worst town in all of China, the Bakers remained there and began to let the light of the Gospel shine through them.

They became quite aware of the teenage beggar boys starving and dying in the streets and decided to open the Adullam Home, an orphanage where these young men received food, clean clothes—and Jesus.

There were 40 boys in Adullam Home when a great miracle took place—the Holy Spirit was poured out strongly upon these teenage boys. Falling under the power of God, they saw into the next world and visited Heaven. H.A. Baker recounted their visions and the glories they saw.[9]

The City of God

The Bible tells us that the future home of God's people is *"the third heaven"* (see 2 Cor. 12:2), a city named the New Jerusalem, whose foundation was laid by God Himself. It is a foursquare city, according to the Bible, and is fifteen hundred miles on every side, surrounded by a wall two hundred feet high with foundations of twelve types of precious stones. The wall itself is made of jasper and has twelve gates that lead into the city, whose streets are like gold.

The children of Adullam were caught up in a vision to this city of God. Their visits were so real that the children thought their souls had left their bodies to go to Heaven and return. Often when they were in Heaven, they gathered extra of the heavenly fruit to bring back to earth for Pastor and Mrs. Baker.

These teenagers seemed to realize that they were only visiting Heaven and would soon return to earth. On returning, they searched for the fruit in their pockets and were surprised to find that the fruit was not there. The boys constantly emphasized that what they saw in their visions was just as real as what they saw on earth, but much clearer because of the light in Heaven.

The Chinese teenagers passed through the first heaven, feeling the air upon their faces. Passing through the second heaven, they saw the stars as from a great height. But as they approached the third Heaven, they saw the lights of the heavenly city and the walls radiating the jasper light. The foundations reflected the light of the beautiful jewels composing them.

They saw this heavenly city as actually three cities in one, with one suspended above another, the largest below, and the smallest on top, similar to a pyramid. Bible students have often thought that the heavenly city is not a cube, but a pyramid; the boys of Adullam knew nothing of this at the time of their visions.

Entering through the pearly gates into a city of golden streets, the boys encountered angels in white who guarded the gates and welcomed those coming into the city. Within this city there was no sorrow, only unspeakable joy. Angels filled the city, ready to escort the children from one place to another and to explain to them all they did not understand.

Often, the angels gave the children harps and taught them to sing and play and also how to blow trumpets and taught them the music and language of Heaven. On earth, the children could be observed to dance, with eyes closed, in perfect rhythm around the room; in their visions, they were dancing with the angels and keeping time to the heavenly music. Frequently the children could be heard singing new songs they had never been taught.

At times, three or four boys would go off to themselves under the power of the Holy Spirit and sing heavenly hymns, accompanied by trumpets and harps. They frequently sang in angelic languages unless they had decided to sing a hymn from earth, which they would sing in Chinese.

But the climax of their visions was seeing Jesus and worshiping Him. After entering the gates of the city, the children were escorted by angels to see Jesus. As they came into His presence, they stood reverently, looking with love and devotion upon Him. First they would thank Him, worshiping and bowing down before Him. Then they entered into true worship of Him as they bowed down to the floor.

The children saw Christ's throne just as it appeared to John on the Island of Patmos in Revelation 4:2-5. They saw the rainbow around the throne and the four and twenty elders seated, clothed in white clothing, with crowns of gold upon their heads. While the children were always thrilled at the golden streets and the presence of the angels, Jesus remained the center of their devotion. His name was mentioned in all their conversations, and His praise was constantly spoken.

On each side of the golden streets were buildings with a room for each person, with every room opening onto the street. There were precious jewels on the doors and around the front of the buildings. Angels led the children into the rooms, where the names of the occupants appeared above each door. Each room had the same type of furnishings: a golden table with a Bible, a flower vase, a pen, and a book. Next to the table was a golden chair, and there was a golden bed with a golden chest. Each room contained a crown of jewels, a golden harp, and a trumpet. Even the walls were made of gold! Light shown forth from the Bible with such brilliance that the room needed no other light. Visitors were told that when they came to stay after their earthly deaths, they could pick any flowers they wished to place in the vases.

During their visits in Heaven, the children could go to their rooms whenever they wished to read their Bibles or play with their harps and trumpets. Frequently, they took their harps and trumpets into the streets to play and sing with the angels and the redeemed.

The boys seemed to know that these were just temporary visits to Heaven and that they would be returning to earth to tell others what they had seen. However, while in Heaven, each one would call the others to come see the room the Lord had prepared for him, and they rejoiced together.

On the very first day of the visits to Heaven, one boy was taken up and greeted by angels and two Adullam boys who had died the year before. With them was a little girl who had died about four years earlier. These who had gone on before led the "newcomers" around Heaven, first of all to see Jesus so they could thank and worship Him. They were given white garments, similar to those of the angels. The angels, however, had wings,

which the redeemed did not have. There was a definite distinc-
tion between the two.

As more of the Adullam children visited Heaven, they
saw the two boys who had died the year before. The two boys
who had died did not seem far away—just out of sight. Heaven
seemed so real and wonderful that if any of the Adullam boys
had died at that time, the others would have envied him being
there. Heaven became real and near to the beggar children of
the Adullam Home!

Chapter Twenty-Four

THE PARADISE OF GOD

THE BIBLE REVEALS THAT HEAVEN is also known as *paradise* (see Luke 23:43). It is a place planned for mankind's eternal happiness. Man's sin, however, has caused him to lose his relationship with God and his place in paradise.

The children of Adullam had never been taught about paradise before their visions of Heaven. Rather, as they returned, they began to teach H.A. Baker and his wife about paradise!

The paradise the children saw was like a great "park" filled with wonder. The word *paradise* in the Bible means a place of pleasure or delight. However, the "park" in Heaven is only somewhat like a park on earth; it is much larger and more beautiful than any earthly park.

One of the boys who visited paradise met two Adullam boys there who had died earlier. They led him through paradise, coming to a great open plot of lawn surrounded by magnificent trees. The scene was so marvelous that the boy told his two friends that he would stay there as there could be nothing more beautiful!

But his two friends told him that there were even greater sights to behold.

Continuing a little farther, they came to even more wonderful trees, some of which bore fruit. The surroundings and the grassy lawn far surpassed anything on earth. Again, the young man told them he would stay there—it was so beautiful that he could not stand to leave it.

No, his friends said. There were greater things yet in Heaven. Still, he stayed there, and his two friends left him on the velvet-like grassy lawn, where his soul was flooded with joy. At various times an angel would pass by, playing a harp and singing. The angel offered the boy his harp, but he declined, protesting that he could not play it. Other angels passed by, smiling as they played and sang. The boy of Adullam said he could not begin to describe the beauty of an angel's smile.

In paradise, the boys saw trees bearing delicious fruit, beautiful expanses of fragrant flowers, exotically colored birds with their glorious songs, and animals of all sorts, both familiar animals such as deer, lions, elephants, and rabbits, and those they had never seen before. They even climbed upon a lion's back, ran their fingers through his mane, and put their hands in his mouth! There was no hostility or danger there.

When they became hungry, the boys ate delicious fruit or the manna that was scattered around. If they were thirsty, there were numerous refreshing brooks filled with the water of life.

In the open grassy areas between the groves of trees, the children of Adullam saw companies of the redeemed dancing and playing trumpets with the angels. They frequently joined this group composed of younger and older children and adults, although no one was marked by age. The angels pointed out to them Abraham, David, Daniel, the prophets, martyrs of old,

James, Peter, John, and many other saints. One boy saw his aunt and his little sister who had preceded him to the "other side."

One boy was given a vision of what happened at the death of a Christian. While relatives and friends gathered around the deathbed on earth, an angel stood nearby awaiting the liberation of the soul. When the soul was finally set free from the body, the angel took him by the arm and ascended with him into Heaven. The powers of darkness in the mid-heavens attempted to hinder the passage of the angel and his charge but could not; they were overcome by the angel's faith and praises to God.

Welcomed at the gate, the new arrival was received by hosts of angels, singing, dancing, rejoicing, and united in giving him a "royal welcome." The visions of the boys of Adullam have confirmed the promises of God's Word concerning the eternal life to be found in Jesus Christ.

H.A. Baker remained in China until the communist takeover, when he fled to Formosa (modern-day Taiwan). He remained there until his death in 1971, and was buried in Li Shan, Miaoli, next to his wife.

Chapter Twenty-Five

YOU CAN SEE HEAVEN

THERE IS A REAL, LITERAL Heaven. Fifty-three of the 66 books of the Bible mention it directly, and even in those 13 which do not, the principles and concepts found there are in agreement with the idea of an actual place called Heaven.

Heaven is first of all the place where God lives. Yet, even it is not large enough to contain Him, as King Solomon knew when he built the first temple for God here on earth.

But will God really dwell on earth? The heavens, even the highest heaven, cannot contain You. How much less this temple I have built! (1 Kings 8:27 NIV)

Things on earth are shadows of what is found in Heaven. Moses was given the details of the tabernacle, or "tent of meeting," that God wanted him to build in the wilderness. This tabernacle was the forerunner of the temple Solomon built later. Moses was told that it was patterned on the heavenly tabernacle, which God had built.

They serve at a sanctuary that is a copy and shadow of what is in heaven. This is why Moses was warned when he was about to build the tabernacle: "See to it that you make everything according to the pattern shown you on the mountain" (Hebrews 8:5 NIV).

Psalm 102:19 says that the Lord looks down on the earth *"from the height of His sanctuary; from heaven did the Lord behold the earth."* Heaven is so taken for granted as the place where God lives that writers of the books of the Bible, under inspiration of the Holy Spirit, often use Heaven and God interchangeably. In Luke 15:18, the prodigal son said, *"I have sinned against heaven* [God]."

What I saw in Heaven might not be the same as that described by someone else who also had the privilege of visiting there and then returning to earth. That is because Heaven is such a vast place, and all of it is not shown to any one person anymore than a brief visitor to the United States could tell you what the East, North, South, West, Southwest, Midwest, and so forth are all like.

What is important is that God is *real,* He lives in a real place, and we will be in that real place when we arrive at His home. We will have perfected bodies that never grow old or become sick. Our bodies will be made of the particular material that comprises the supernatural realm, just as God created our natural bodies from the dust of this earth.

You have already seen that people walk, talk, have houses, and eat in Heaven—not just from my vision, but from Scriptures I have quoted in this book. You have seen there are lands, streets, towns, countryside, rivers, and streams. There are flowers and trees, animals and birds in Heaven.

Unbelievers, you *already* have eternal life. No spirit being apparently can ever die or cease its existence, according to the Bible. The issue in question, however, is *where* you will spend the rest of your eternal life. Where will you be during that unending forever, once this brief span of life on earth—as brief as the snap of your fingers compared to eternity—is finished?

The terms "converted" or "saved" mean the same thing. A person has turned from sin to God and now belongs to Him. These saved people have put their trust in Jesus' sacrifice on the cross for their sins and have chosen to live for Him. They are now God's children, and Heaven is their destination.

But being saved is more than a simple decision to "turn over a new leaf." When you give your life to Jesus Christ and allow Him to be the rightful Lord of your whole being, you become a new person. In John 3:3, Jesus said that to see Heaven, we must be born again. Second Corinthians 5:17 explains this further, saying that if any man or woman is in Christ, they are a new creation. The old has passed and the new has come.

How does this take place? How can you be born again and have Heaven in your future?

First, you must recognize that you have sinned against God and need His salvation. Romans 3:23 declares that all have sinned and fallen short of God's glory.

Second, you must realize that there is only one Savior, Jesus, who is the only way to God. In John 14:6, Jesus said, *"I am the way, the truth, and the life. No man comes to the Father except by me."*

Third, Jesus has the right to be Lord of your entire life. You must receive Him as Lord by first believing that He was raised from the dead and by speaking with your mouth that He is now your Lord. Romans 10:9-10 says:

If you confess with your mouth, "Jesus is Lord," and believe in your heart that God raised him from the dead, you will be saved. For it is with your heart that you believe and are justified, and it is with your mouth that you confess and are saved (NIV).

If you want to be born again and receive this salvation and the assurance of living eternally with Jesus in Heaven, then pray this prayer from a sincere heart:

Lord, forgive me of all my sins. You said that if we were quick to confess our sins, You would be faithful to forgive (see 1 John 1:9). You sent Your only begotten Son to die on the cross at Calvary two thousand years ago because You loved us so much (see John 3:16). So I know that if I ask Jesus to be my Lord—as I do right now—He will come into my heart and live with me. Jesus, I believe You are the only way to God the Father, and I receive You now as my Lord, Savior, Healer, Deliverer, and High Priest. You are King of kings and Lord of lords, and I want to give my life to You as You gave Your life for me. I want You to be my best friend forever, and I will serve You all the days of this life and throughout eternity. Amen.

Now that you have made this decision, there are some things that you can do to begin your growth as a believer.

First, tell someone that you have made Jesus your Lord and that He has become your Savior. In Romans 10:9, the apostle Paul tells us to confess with our mouth that Jesus is Lord. You can also write to us at Roberts Liardon Ministries. We want to know of your new life in Christ!

Our address is:
Roberts Liardon Ministries
PO Box 2989
Sarasota, FL 34230

You may wish to visit our Website at: www.robertsliardon. org. You can also email us about your decision to follow Jesus. I want to send you some material that will help you begin your walk with God.

Second, find a local church where the full Gospel is believed and taught, a church that believes the Bible is the inspired Word of God. You will need to tell the pastor that you have asked Christ into your heart and that you need to be water baptized, according to Mark 16:16. There is no substitute for fellowship in a local church and for being pastored by a man or woman who cares about the children of God in their congregation.

Finally, get a version of the Bible that you feel comfortable reading. Most towns of any size have Christian bookstores, and even shopping mall bookstore chains usually have a shelf with Bibles. The *King James Version* is the traditional English version, and the *New King James Version* has replaced words like "thou" and "teacheth" with "you" and "teaches." The New International Version is written in today's English, as is the New American Standard and many others.

For your first study Bible, you are better off with a *translation* rather than a *paraphrase* in a modern language, of which there are several available. No matter how well-intentioned the authors are, any *paraphrase* is simply someone's opinion of what the *King James Version* means. A *translation* uses the English word that best translates, or is a counterpart of, a Hebrew or Greek word.

God bless you in your decision to follow Christ's leading and fulfill His purpose on earth for your life. Not only will you begin to experience what John 10:10 in *The Living Bible* calls *"life in all its fullness,"* but you are assured that someday you, too, will see Heaven!

WHAT THE BIBLE SAYS...

What the Bible Says about Heaven

ALTHOUGH THE BIBLE DOES NOT tell us every possible detail about Heaven, it nonetheless describes quite clearly many aspects of it. I want you to see for yourself what God's Word tells us about the place God has prepared for His people!

Are there animals in Heaven?

Yes, for Second Kings 2:11 tells of the fiery horses drawing the chariot that took the prophet Elijah up into Heaven: *"There appeared a chariot of fire, and horses of fire, and parted them both asunder; and Elijah went up by a whirlwind into heaven."* In addition, Revelation 4:7 speaks of the four beasts, three of which are like a lion, a calf, and a flying eagle. Revelation 6:2-8 tells of the four horsemen, seated variously upon a white, a red, a black, and a pale horse. Revelation 19:17 mentions, *"all the fowls that fly in the midst of heaven."*

Are there trees in Heaven?

Revelation 7:9 tells of palms, obviously from palm trees, and Revelation 22:2 refers to the tree of life, its fruit and its leaves.

What beings are in Heaven?

God is there, for Second Chronicles 6:18 says that Heaven is His dwelling place, and Deuteronomy 26:15 reveals it to be His holy habitation. Jesus is there because Hebrews 9:24 says He has entered into Heaven itself and appears in God's presence for us now; and the Holy Spirit is there according to John 1:32 where John the Baptist saw Him descending from Heaven like a dove.

In addition to the Godhead, angels are there according to Revelation 8:10 and 8:13 and are referred to in many places such as Deuteronomy 17:3 as the host of Heaven. Revelation 5:13 refers to *"every creature which is in heaven,"* and Philippians 2:10 speaks of every knee, of things in Heaven, bowing to the name of Jesus.

And, of course, there are the believers who now dwell in Heaven, according to Hebrews 12:23, who are referred to as *"the general assembly and church of the firstborn"* and *"the spirits of just men made perfect."* Ephesians 3:15 calls them the *"family in heaven."* Psalm 89:6 makes it clear that none of the others beings in Heaven can even compare with God!

Is there marriage in Heaven?

Jesus said, in Matthew 22:30, *"For in the resurrection they neither marry, nor are given in marriage, but are as the angels of God in heaven."*

Are there buildings in Heaven?

In John 14:2a, Jesus said, *"In my Father's house are many mansions."* Hebrews 8:2 and 9:11 speak of Christ serving in the "true" or "more perfect tabernacle," which is in Heaven. Revelation 11:1 reveals that the temple of God is in Heaven. Psalm 102:19 says that His sanctuary is in Heaven.

Are there streets in Heaven?

Revelation 22:1-2 says, *"Then the angel showed me the river of the water of life, as clear as crystal, flowing from the throne of God and of the Lamb down the middle of the great street of the city..."* (NIV). Revelation 21:21 reveals that those streets are made of gold, as transparent as glass.

Are there bodies of water in Heaven?

Revelation 4:6 tells of a sea like crystal; Revelation 7:17 speaks of fountains of waters; and Revelation 22:1-2 describes the river of the water of life.

What do angels do in Heaven?

Revelation 4:8 says that they cry, *"Holy, holy, holy."* Revelation 8:13 describes an angel flying, crying, *"Woe"* three times; and Revelation 14:6 says another angel flies with the everlasting Gospel. In Revelation 15:6-7, there are angels with gold girdles holding golden vials. Revelation 4:10 says that the angels bow down and worship God.

Where is the river in Heaven and what is it like?

It flows from the throne of God and of the Lamb down the middle of the great street of the city, according to Revelation 22:1-2, which describes it as clear as crystal.

What is God's throne like?

First, Psalm 11:4 tells us that His throne is in Heaven, and Isaiah 66:1 says that Heaven is His throne. Revelation 4:2 reveals that the throne is set in Heaven and that One sits upon it. Revelation 20:11 describes it as a *"great white throne."*

Are there laws in Heaven?

Jeremiah 33:25 says, *"Thus saith the Lord; If my covenant be not with day and night, and if I have not appointed the ordinances [laws] of heaven and earth."* The Lord's prayer in Matthew 6:10 declares, *"Thy Kingdom come. Thy will [law] be done in earth, as it is in heaven."*

How may a person be little or great in Heaven?

In Matthew 5:19, Jesus said, *"Whosoever therefore shall break one of these least commandments, and shall teach men so, he shall be called the least in the kingdom of heaven: but whosoever shall do and teach them, the same shall be called great in the kingdom of heaven."* He further told the disciples in Matthew 23:11, that *"He that is greatest among you shall be your servant."*

Are there armies and war in Heaven?

Daniel 4:35 mentions the army of Heaven; Revelation 12:7 tells of war in Heaven with Michael and his angels fighting the dragon, or satan; and Revelation 19:14a says, *"And the armies which were in heaven followed him upon white horses."*

Is there clothing in Heaven?

Revelation 19:14 also describes the clothing in Heaven. The riders were *"dressed in fine linen, white and clean"*. Revelation 7:9 describes 144,000 saying, *"They were wearing white robes and were holding palm branches in their hands"* (NIV).

Is there food in Heaven?

Revelation 19:9 tells of the great marriage supper: *"Blessed are those who are invited to the wedding supper of the Lamb!"* (NIV).

Is there darkness in Heaven?

There is no darkness in Heaven because, according to Revelation 21:23,25, there is no need of sun nor is there night because the *"Lamb is the light thereof."*

How big is Heaven?

First Kings 8:27 says, *"...the heaven and heaven of heavens cannot contain thee* [God].*"* Isaiah 66:1 says that *"Heaven is My throne, and the earth is My footstool. Where is the house you will build for Me? Where will My resting place be?"* (NIV). Whatever size we might consider Heaven to be, God fills it completely!

Are there books in Heaven?

Books are certainly implied as being in Heaven according to Hebrews 12:23, which speaks of the general assembly and church of the firstborn, *"which are written in heaven,"* and Revelation 20:12 and 21:27 talk about books being opened and the *"book of life"* and the *"Lamb's book of life."* Revelation 10:2 tells of a *"little book."* In Luke 10:20, Jesus speaks of our names being written in Heaven. Revelation 5:1 talks of the book with the seven seals.

Are there emotions in Heaven?

Luke 15:7 says that there is joy in Heaven over even one sinner who repents. Luke 19:38 speaks of peace in Heaven. Romans 1:18a says, *"For the wrath of God is revealed from Heaven against all ungodliness."* Colossians 1:5 says that there is hope laid up for us in Heaven.

What is the attitude in Heaven toward God's Word?

Psalm 119:89 says, *"For ever, O Lord, thy word is settled in heaven,"* and Matthew 24:35 declares that, *"Heaven and earth shall pass away, but my words shall not pass away."*

Are there doors in Heaven?

Revelation 4:1 speaks of a door that opens in Heaven.

Are clouds and harps in Heaven?

Revelations 14:2b suggests that there are harps, saying, *"The sound I heard was like that of harpists playing their harps"* (NIV). Further on in the chapter, in verse 14, *"I looked, and there before me was a white cloud, and seated on the cloud was one 'like a son of man' with a crown of gold on his head and a sharp sickle in his hand."* It does not seem, however, that harp playing is all we will do, nor is anyone but Jesus on a cloud!

Is there sound in Heaven?

There is much sound in Heaven! Revelation 14:2-3 speaks of sound like the roaring of rushing waters and like a loud peal of thunder, and of a sound like harpists playing their harps. A "new song" is sung, and the angels cry out and speak in loud voices (see Rev. 14:9 among others). Yet, there is also silence in Heaven for about one-half hour, according to Revelation 8:1. Many Scriptures, such as Genesis 22:15, indicate that God calls to mankind or to individuals out of Heaven.

Is there furniture in Heaven?

In addition to God's throne (see Psalm 11:4), Revelation 1:13 speaks of furniture; Revelation 4:4 speaks of the chairs for the four and twenty elders; Revelation 6:9 tells of the altar; and Revelation 8:3 calls it a gold altar with a gold censor upon it. The ark of His testament is also there, according to Revelation 11:19.

What ascends into Heaven and what descends from or goes out of it?

According to Genesis 22:15, among many other passages, God's voice calls out of Heaven. According to Second Chronicles

6:21, God also hears out of Heaven and forgives. In Genesis 28:12, Jacob dreamed of a ladder reaching to Heaven with the angels of God ascending and descending on it. According to Psalm 33:13, the Lord looks down out of Heaven; and in Psalm 57:3, we find that He sends from Heaven to save us. Isaiah 14:12 tells of the fall of lucifer out of Heaven. In John 1:51, Jesus said that we would see Heaven open and the angels of God ascending and descending upon the Son of man.

In John 6:32, Jesus said that He was the true bread given from Heaven by God. Acts 1:11 says that Jesus was taken up into Heaven, and First Peter 3:22 says He has gone into Heaven and is on the right hand of God with the angels and authorities and powers subjected to Him. First Thessalonians 4:16 says that, *"The Lord himself shall descend from heaven with a shout, with the voice of the archangel, and with the trump of God...."* Revelation 3:12 reveals that the New Jerusalem will come down out of Heaven from God, and Revelation 20:9 speaks of the fire of God coming down from Heaven.

From where did Heaven come and to whom does it belong?

Genesis 1:1 and Second Kings 19:15, among others, reveal that Heaven came from God, who made it. Genesis 14:22 calls God the *"possessor of heaven."*

What will not be in Heaven?

Revelation 21:4 says that God will wipe away all tears and there will be no death, mourning, crying, or pain in Heaven. Revelation 21:8 says, *"But the cowardly, the unbelieving, the vile, the murderers, the sexually immoral, those who practice magic arts, the idolaters and all liars..."* (NIV) will not be in Heaven. He promises that those who will be in Heaven are those who overcome and *"will inherit all this"* (Rev. 21:7 NIV). What a promise!

What are other names for Heaven?

Jesus called Heaven *"my Father's house"* in John 14:2, and Heaven is known as *"paradise"* in Luke 23:43, Second Corinthians 12:4, and Revelation 2:7. Galatians 4:26, Hebrews 12:22, and Revelation 3:12 refer to Heaven as the heavenly Jerusalem; and Second Peter 1:11 (NIV) calls it *"the eternal kingdom."* First Peter 1:4 and Hebrews 9:15 call Heaven the eternal inheritance. Hebrews 11:14,16 refer to it as the *"better country,"* and both Matthew 25:1 and James 2:5 speak of Heaven as *"the kingdom of heaven."*

To what is the Kingdom of Heaven compared?

It is compared to a man who sowed good seed in Matthew 13:24-30,38-43 and Mark 4:26-29; to a grain of mustard seed in Matthew 13:31-32, Mark 4:30-31 and Luke 13:18-19; and to leaven (yeast) in Matthew 13:33 and Luke 13:21. It is also compared to a treasure in Matthew 13:44; to a *"pearl of great price"* in Matthew 13:46; and to a net in Matthew 13:47-50. The Kingdom of Heaven is likened to a king who called his servants for a reckoning (an audit) in Matthew 18:23-35; and to a householder in Matthew 20:1-16; and to a king who held a marriage feast for his son in Matthew 22:2-14 and Luke 14:16-24. Finally, it is compared to ten virgins in Matthew 25:1-13 and to a man traveling into a far country, who called his servants together and handed over his goods to them in Matthew 25:14-30 and Luke 19:12-27.

What is the Kingdom of Heaven not like?

Jesus said that His Kingdom *"is not of this world"* in John 18:36; and the apostle Paul said in Romans 14:17 that it does not consist of *"meat and drink; but righteousness, and peace, and joy in the Holy Ghost."*

What the Bible Says about Hell

Does hell exist?

Yes, according to the story of the beggar and the rich man, *"...The rich man also died and was buried. In hell, where he was in torment, he looked up and saw Abraham far away, with Lazarus by his side"* (Luke 16:22-23 NIV).

Are there torments in hell?

Luke again answers the question: *"In hell, where he was in torment, he looked up and saw Abraham far away, with Lazarus by his side"* (Luke 16:23 NIV).

Does God send people to hell?

God desires that none would perish (see Matt. 18:14). He tells us in Second Timothy 2:25-26, *"Those who oppose him he must gently instruct, in the hope that God will grant them repentance leading them to a knowledge of the truth, and that they will come to their senses and escape from the trap of the devil, who has taken them captive to do his will"* (NIV).

Do people want to escape hell?

Yes. The torture in hell is unlike anything on earth. Returning to the story in Luke 16 about the rich man in hell, *"So he called to him, 'Father Abraham, have pity on me and send Lazarus to dip the tip of his finger in water and cool my tongue, because I am in agony in this fire.' But Abraham replied, 'Son, remember that in your lifetime you received your good things, while Lazarus received bad things, but now he is comforted here and you are in agony'"* (Luke 16:24-25 NIV).

Can people escape hell?

No; as evidenced by Abraham's response to the rich man who was in agony in hell, *"And besides all this, between us and* you a great chasm has been fixed, so that those who want to go from here to you cannot, nor can anyone cross over from there to us" (Luke 16:26 NIV).

What condemns people to hell?

Matthew is very clear that sin causes people to go to hell, *"If your right eye causes you to sin, gouge it out and throw it away. It is better for you to lose one part of your body than for your whole body to be thrown into hell"* (Matthew 5:29 NIV). See also Matthew 5:30 where he states the same thing about "your right hand."

Mark is just a clear, *"And if your foot causes you to sin, cut it off. It is better for you to enter life crippled than to have two feet and be thrown into hell"* (Mark 9:45 NIV).

Are there horrors in hell?

The psalmist prayed to God to *"Haul my betrayers off alive to hell—let them experience the horror, let them feel every desolate detail of a damned life"* (Psalm 55:15 MSG).

Did God spare the angels that sinned?

No; *"For if God did not spare angels when they sinned, but sent them to hell, putting them into gloomy dungeons to be held for judgment"* (2 Peter 2:4 NIV).

What happens to the wicked who forget God?

According to the psalmist, *"The wicked return to the grave, all the nations that forget God"* (Psalm 9:17 NIV).

What actions take a person to the brink of hell's fire?

Jesus tells us in that even speaking hurtful words can lead us to hell, *"You're familiar with the command to the ancients,*

'Do not murder.' I'm telling you that anyone who is so much as angry with a brother or sister is guilty of murder. Carelessly call a brother 'idiot!' and you just might find yourself hauled into court. Thoughtlessly yell 'stupid!' at a sister and you are on the brink of hellfire. The simple moral fact is that words kill" (Matthew 5:22 MSG).

What happens to people who don't live for God?

The psalmist is clear about what happens to those who don't accept Jesus Christ as Lord and Savior, *"This is what happens to those who live for the moment, who only look out for themselves: Death herds them like sheep straight to hell; they disappear down the gullet of the grave; They waste away to nothing—nothing left but a marker in a cemetery"* (Psalm 49:13-15 MSG).

What is the lake of fire?

John reveals that the lake of fire is real, *"Then death and Hades were thrown into the lake of fire. The lake of fire is the second death"* (Revelation 20:14 NIV).

What happens to a person whose name is not in the Book of Life?

"If anyone's name was not found written in the book of life, he was thrown into the lake of fire" (Revelation 20:15 NIV).

Additional Scriptures Concerning Heaven

These passages identify Heaven as God's dwelling place (Nave's Topical Bible, on the Internet at: www.biblestudytools. net/Concordances/Naves Topical Bible). In addition to examining these passages, you may wish to do further study about Heaven. The following Scripture references will help you as you look further into God's Word for revelation concerning the true home and hope of every believer!

- Deuteronomy 26:15

- 1 Kings 8:30,39,43,49

- 1 Chronicles 16:31; 21:26

- 2 Chronicles 2:6; 6:18,21,27

- Nehemiah 9:27

- Job 22:12,14

- Psalms 2:4; 11:4; 20:6; 33:13; 102:19; 103:19; 113:5; 123:1; 135:6

- Ecclesiastes 5:2

- Isaiah 2:1-5; 57:15; 63:15; 66:1

- Jeremiah 23:24

- Lamentations 3:41,50

- Daniel 4:35; 5:23

- Zechariah 2:13

- Matthew 5:34,45; 6:9; 10:32-33; 11:25; 12:50; 13:33; 16:17; 18:19

- Mark 11:25-26; 16:19

- Acts 7:49

- Romans 1:18

- Hebrews 8:1

- Revelation 8:1; 12:7-9; 21:22-27

Other Names for Heaven

In addition to being the habitation for God, Heaven is also referred to in the following Scriptures as the future dwelling place of the righteous, those who have been bought with the blood of Jesus.

- It is called a garner (KJV) or barn (NIV) in Matthew 3:12:

  "His winnowing fork is in his hand, and he will clear his threshing floor, gathering his wheat into the barn and burning up the chaff with unquenchable fire" (NIV).

- Heaven is called the Kingdom of Christ and of God in Ephesians 5:5:

  "No immoral, impure or greedy person—such a man is an idolator—has any inheritance in the kingdom of Christ and of God" (NIV).

- It is called the Father's house in John 14:2:

  "In My Father's house are many rooms; if it were not so, I would have told you. I am going there to prepare a place for you" (NIV).

- It is known as a heavenly country in Hebrews 11:16:

  "Instead, they were longing for a better country—a heavenly one. Therefore God is not ashamed to be called their God, for he has prepared a city for them" (NIV).

- Both Hebrews 4:9 and Revelation 14:13 call it a rest:

  "There remains, then, a Sabbath-rest for the people of God" (NIV).

*"...they will rest from their labor, for their deeds will fol-
low them"* (NIV).

• Heaven is also named paradise in Second Corinthians 12:3-4a:

*"And I know that this man—whether in the body or
apart from the body I do not know, but God knows—was
caught up to paradise"* (NIV).

• Galatians 5:21, Ephesians 5:5, and Revelation 22:15
  indicate that the wicked are excluded from Heaven,

*"I warn you, as I did before, that those who live like this
will not inherit the kingdom of God"* (NIV).

*"No immoral, impure or greedy person...has any inheri-
tance in the kingdom of Christ and of God"* (NIV).

*"Outside are...those who practice magic arts, the sexu-
ally immoral, the murderers, the idolaters and everyone
who loves and practices falsehood"* (NIV).

Other Passages Referring to Heaven

2 Kings 2:11 — The prophet Elijah is taken to Heaven in a
whirlwind by a fiery horse and chariot.

Job 3:17 — Heaven is the place where the weary are at rest.

Psalm 16:11 — Heaven is the place of joy and eternal
pleasures.

Psalm 17:15 — Believers will see God's face there and be sat-
isfied with seeing His likeness.

Psalm 23:6 — It is called the *"house of the Lord,"* where
believers will dwell forever.

Psalm 24:3,7 — Heaven is God's holy place, and it is where the King of Glory enters.

Psalm 73:24 — Heaven is referred to as His "glory."

Isaiah 33:17 (NIV) — It is a land that *"stretches afar."*

Isaiah 49:3,10 — Heaven is described as a place where God's people will find pasture and neither hunger nor thirst, a place with springs of water.

Daniel 12:3 — The wise are compared to the brightness of Heaven.

Malachi 3:17 (NIV) — It is the place of God's *"treasured possession."*

Matthew 3:12 — Heaven is where God will gather His people.

Matthew 5:3,10,12,20 — It is His Kingdom, where His people will receive their reward and where only the righteous may enter.

Matthew 6:20 — We can store up treasure there, where it will not be destroyed.

Matthew 8:11 — Heaven is also known as the *"kingdom of heaven,"* where there will be a great feast for those God has gathered there.

Matthew 13:30,43,49 (NIV) – It is compared to a barn where precious grain is gathered and a place where the righteous will "shine like the sun."

Matthew 18:10 — In Heaven, the guardian angels look upon God's face.

Matthew 19:21 — Jesus told the "rich young ruler" to sell all he had and follow Him, in order to have treasure in Heaven.

Matthew 25:34,46 — At God's right hand in Heaven will be those who are *"blessed of my Father,"* and they will have eternal life.

Luke 10:20 — The names of believers are written in Heaven.

Luke 12:8,32-33 — It is where the angels of God dwell, and it is His Kingdom, where we can lay up treasure.

Luke 15:6-7,10,32 — In Heaven, there is rejoicing over the salvation of the lost, over the sinner who repents, and over the lost who is found.

Luke 16:22 (NIV) — Heaven is also called *"Abraham's bosom"* or *"Abraham's side."*

Luke 20:34-36 — It is called the *"resurrection from the dead"* where there is no marriage and there is no death.

Luke 22:29-30 — Heaven is Jesus' Kingdom where His saints will sit at His table.

Luke 23:43 — It is called *"paradise,"* where we will be with Him.

John 5:28-29 — The day is coming when those in their graves will come out of them; the good will go to life and the evil to condemnation.

John 10:28 — The place of eternal life, where no one can snatch us out of Jesus' hand.

John 12:26 — It is the place where Jesus and His servants will be.

John 13:36 — It is the place to where we will follow Jesus.

John 14:2-3 — It is the Father's house, where there are many rooms—and one of them is being prepared for each of us.

John 17:22,24 — Heaven is where Jesus is, where He and the Father are one, and from where He sends His glory upon the Church.

Acts 7:55-56 — Stephen looked up into Heaven and saw Jesus standing at God's right hand.

Romans 5:17 — The place where believers will reign through Jesus Christ.

2 Corinthians 5:1 (NIV) — Our *"eternal house."*

2 Corinthians 12:2-4 — Heaven is also referred to as the *"third heaven,"* the place where God dwells.

Ephesians 1:18 — Heaven is called our glorious inheritance.

Colossians 1:5-6,12 — It is the place where our hope is stored up and is a Kingdom of light.

Colossians 3:4 — Heaven is where we will appear with Christ in glory.

1 Thessalonians 4:17 — Heaven is the place to which we will be caught up to meet the Lord.

2 Thessalonians 1:7-8 — It is the place from which Jesus is revealed in blazing fire with His angels.

2 Thessalonians 2:14 — Heaven is where we will share in the glory of the Lord Jesus.

Hebrews 10:34 (NIV) — It is the place of our *"better and lasting possessions."*

Hebrews 11:10,16 (NIV) — Heaven is the city prepared for us without foundations, *"whose architect and builder is God."*

Hebrews 12:22-24,28 — We will come to the heavenly Jerusalem, the city of God, where thousands of angels joyfully assemble in the unshakable Kingdom.

Hebrews 13:14 — Heaven is the city which is to come.

1 Peter 1:4 — It is the location of our imperishable inheritance.

2 Peter 1:11 (NIV) — Heaven is the eternal Kingdom of Jesus Christ where we will receive a *"rich welcome."*

2 Peter 3:13 (NIV) — It is the *"home of righteousness."*

Revelation 2:7 — The tree of life is in Heaven, in the *"paradise of God."*

Revelation 3:21 — It is where the throne of God the Father and the Lord Jesus Christ are.

Revelation 4:4 — The throne of God is surrounded by the thrones of the 24 elders.

Revelation 5:9 — It is where the 24 elders and the four creatures will sing *"a new song"* to God.

Revelation 7:9,13-17 — The great multitude of the redeemed from every nation will be in Heaven, where we will serve Him day and night, never hungering, thirsting, or sorrowing.

Revelation 14:1-3 (NIV) — In Heaven, there will come a sound like the *"roar of rushing waters."*

Revelation 15:2 — There will be a sea like glass in Heaven, mixed with fire, and around it will be those who have overcome the enemy.

Revelation 20:1-5,9-15 — From Heaven will come the angel who will lock the devil in the abyss. Within Heaven will be a great white throne, where the dead will be judged according to their deeds on earth.

Revelation 22:1-5 (NIV) — The river of the *"water of life"* is in Heaven, and it is clear as crystal. It flows from the throne of God and of the Lamb down the middle of a great street. On each side of the river is the tree of life, which bears 12 crops of fruit, one for each month. The leaves of that tree are to heal the nations of the world. There will be neither curse nor darkness in Heaven. God will reign there forever and ever!

As you study God's Word for yourself, you will begin to see the glories of Heaven in your own life. The Bible really does reveal to us that Heaven exists and that it has been prepared for those who have believed on Jesus Christ and put their faith in His work at the cross. We have much to look forward to in our eternal home with Him!

ENDNOTES

1. A "false vision," that is, one not from God, is mentioned in Jeremiah 14:14 and 23:16.

2. Kenneth E. Hagin, *I Believe in Visions* (Scottsdale, AZ: Faith Library Publications, 1984). (Publications of Dr. Lester Sumrall and Norvel Hayes are also widely available concerning Heaven.)

3. Rebecca Springer, *Within Heaven's Gates* (New Kensington, PA: Whitaker House, 1984).

4. Jesse Duplantis, *Heaven, Close Encounters of the God Kind* (Tulsa, OK: Harrison House, 1996).

5. John Milton, *Paradise Lost* (Gonic, NH: The Odyssey Press, 1999).

6. Roy Hicks, *Guardian Angels: How to Activate Their Ministry in Your Life* (Tulsa, OK: Harrison House, 1999).

7. Marietta Davis, *Caught Up Into Heaven* (New Kensington, PA: Whitaker House, 1999).

8. Rebecca Ruter Springer, *Intra Muros* (Colorado Springs, CO: David C. Cook Publishing Company, 1898).

9. H.A. Baker, *Visions of Heaven* (Minneapolis, MN: Osterhus Publishing House, 1996).

ABOUT ROBERTS LIARDON

Roberts Liardon Ministries

PO Box 2989
Sarasota, FL 34230

Phone: 941-373-3883

Fax: 941-373-3884

Web: www.robertsliardon.com
Twitter: @RobertsLiardon
Facebook: Roberts Liardon Official

Visit the following Website to see rare film footage, photographs, and voice recordings of Smith Wigglesworth, Aimee Semple McPherson, A.A. Allen, Kathryn Kuhlman, and many more:

www.godsgenerals.org

In the right hands, This Book will Change Lives!

Most of the people who need this message will not be looking for this book. To change their lives, you need to put a copy of this book in their hands.

> *But others (seeds) fell into good ground, and brought forth fruit, some a hundred-fold, some sixty-fold, some thirty-fold* (Matthew 13:8).

Our ministry is constantly seeking methods to find the good ground, the people who need this anointed message to change their lives. Will you help us reach these people?

> *Remember this—a farmer who plants only a few seeds will get a small crop. But the one who plants generously will get a generous crop* (2 Corinthians 9:6).

EXTEND THIS MINISTRY BY SOWING
3 BOOKS, 5 BOOKS, 10 BOOKS, OR MORE TODAY,
AND BECOME A LIFE CHANGER!

Thank you,

Don Nori Sr., Founder
Destiny Image
Since 1982

DESTINY IMAGE PUBLISHERS, INC.

"Promoting Inspired Lives."

VISIT OUR NEW SITE HOME AT
WWW.DESTINYIMAGE.COM

FREE SUBSCRIPTION TO DI NEWSLETTER

Receive free unpublished articles by top DI authors, exclusive

discounts, and free downloads from our best and newest books.

Visit www.destinyimage.com to subscribe.

Write to:	Destiny Image
	P.O. Box 310
	Shippensburg, PA 17257-0310
Call:	1-800-722-6774
Email:	orders@destinyimage.com

For a complete list of our titles or to place an order
online, visit www.destinyimage.com.

FIND US ON FACEBOOK OR FOLLOW US ON TWITTER.

www.facebook.com/destinyimage   facebook

www.twitter.com/destinyimage   twitter